BLOOD
IN THE
WATER

AN ACCOUNT OF
WORKPLACE BULLYING

Lynn Hamilton

To my daughter who, when she's old enough to read and understand this book, I hope will learn from it and prevent any of this from happening to herself.

NOTE TO THE READER

The contents of this book relate to personal experiences with workplace harassment and violence. The events and emotions may be triggering.

CONTENTS

PRELUDE

October 2016

MY SECOND ANXIETY attack was coming.

Much like the first one, I felt a flood of anxiety that badly needed an outlet. I was sitting on the bus, waiting to get off to pick up my daughter from school. My supervisor's words, "The Boss and Director know *everything*," repeated themselves in my head. It scared me. Were the things that she accused me of, mostly unjustified and untrue, shared with people whose opinions mattered to me? People who I wanted to think well of me, but who now didn't because of the lies – lies for which I had no evidence to use in my self-defence. *What do they think of me? Do they believe her? What do I do?*

I tried to hide how these thoughts were impacting me. Who wants to cry on the public bus? I tried to push the emotions down. *Keep it together*, I told myself. *You're on the bus, for goodness sake, and you're going to your daughter's school.*

I tried to breathe. I questioned how rational I was being.

You know you can't do anything about it right now. Just breathe, put this aside for now, get your daughter, then go home.

But the emotions were too powerful to push down.

I got off the bus, tears already welling up, and started walking down the street to the school. Then it hit me. A huge exhale coupled with sobs and tears. I doubled over, hand on my chest, trying to catch my breath as I hyperventilated and cried at the same time. And I still tried to pull it together. I wasn't on the bus anymore but I *was* in the middle of a sidewalk, on a busy street, three blocks from my daughter's school. Never mind not wanting motorists to see me like this – I couldn't let my *four-year-old daughter* see me like this either.

After a few minutes I had composed myself, *again*, and continued walking to the school. I don't know how I looked when I got there, but no one said anything. I was grateful. This was the second anxiety attack. The second doubling over on the street, the second needing-to-pull-myself-together so I could pick up my daughter from school. The first time obviously wasn't a fluke. *Could this happen again?* I needed to figure out what was really going on. I could no longer deny how wrong everything had become and how much it had affected me.

The next day, I called the Employee Assistance Program and asked to be referred to a counsellor.

INTRODUCTION

WE NEED TO talk about psychological abuse and mental health in the workplace. Many of us have stories about the co-worker or boss who screamed at someone in a meeting room, the rumours that were spread about a colleague, the boss who played favourites, or a hard worker who never seemed to get promoted. Some of us may know or have heard of someone who just disappeared one day, hearing only that this person needed a "break." Some stories were big enough to hit the media, including those about bullying at the War Museum and in the Governor General's office. The fact that these stories keep appearing, either in the media or in workplace conversation, implies that we haven't yet figured out how to keep these problems from occurring. To do so, we need to talk about them more openly and widely.

This book is about my experiences with workplace harassment and violence and their impact on my mental health. Everything shared, included quoted conversations, is my honest recollection, though through my lens. I do not pretend that the events I recount are unique: I am far from being the first person to experience these challenges, and I know that I won't be the last. The irony though is that in spite of the fact that I am not *alone* in experiencing these things, I felt *lonely* when they were happening. This is partly because if we talk about being abused in the workplace, then we risk looking like we are complaining or have a vendetta against someone, being retaliated against because we made someone look bad, or being disciplined for violating the confidentiality of the offender, who has a right to learn from and move beyond their actions. If we talk about mental health issues at work, then we risk being seen as less capable than our peers and not tough enough to survive and thrive in the workplace.

But by *not* talking about them, we don't build the support network we need to validate our experiences. Without that validation, we feel alone. We also don't stock the information warehouse with experiences we need to understand the different ways workplace violence happens and its effect on mental health, which is important for figuring out how to prevent it. So, I'm sharing mine so that those with similar experiences feel less alone and, hopefully, lead all of us to solutions.

Let's begin.

Those of us with full-time jobs spend more waking hours with our colleagues than with our families. Some of us are fortunate enough to like the people we work with. We become friends, maybe even feel like family members or become life partners, who stay with us even after we stop working together. We become attached.

Attachments can be good things. They can bring us happiness and a sense of belonging which, at work, can motivate us to show up every day just so we can see them, even if we hate what we do. But they can also open us to pain. Like with non-work attachments, work ones can falter due to disagreements, unmet expectations, or their lack of healthiness in the first place. And with that comes the same kettle of emotions, like heartache and confusion, as when non-work relationships fail.

But there is one difference between work and non-work relationships: unless family is involved, you can usually cut ties with or find ways to avoid the other person in the failed non-work relationship. This is not always so in the workplace: if you're on the same team, you need to work with that person every day, respectfully and professionally, all while dealing with whatever emotions the failed relationship left you with – emotions which wouldn't be so negative or strong if you hadn't formed that attachment, and emotions you could better deal with if you could detach from that person.

This can be particularly difficult where psychological abuse is concerned. Most people agree that psychological abuse is wrong in romantic relationships. However, there are those who accept psychological abuse in the workplace because of the power dynamic involved. In the workplace, you expect and accept that someone will have power over you, such as the power to monitor and evaluate your work, dole out assignments, and decide whether you're fit for a promotion. Therefore, if that someone is unhappy with your performance, it is their job to decide how to manage you because of their rank over you. However, not everyone uses this power respectfully or understands that there should be limits on it.

This power dynamic can also play out between colleagues. Colleagues who jockey for plum assignments or promotions, or who simply want to be favoured by the boss, may engage in attacking another colleague's work, spread gossip to ruin their reputation, or use isolation or harassment to drive them off the team. Managers also have images to create and uphold. They need to look like they're fit to manage a team, which some do by browbeating employees into unsustainable production expectations, behaving aggressively to show they're taking action to resolve a problem, or by denying developmental opportunities and marginalizing those they think might outshine them or are otherwise deemed undeserving of their support.

Again, many people agree that these behaviours are wrong. However, if you have a management structure that refuses to acknowledge it, or even rewards it, then you're in a situation where these behaviours are considered acceptable, maybe even desirable. Those at the head of this structure don't see these managers and colleagues as bullies: instead, they're seen as tough, assertive, action-oriented. Their victims are simply weak, deserve what they get, won't accept their failings, or don't understand the bully's true, kinder motivations.

What also makes this issue difficult to address is that victims aren't a homogeneous group. Individual people react to and deal differently with harassment and workplace violence. Some may not believe that how they were treated qualifies as harassment or violence because it doesn't bother them, or because they expect that behaviour to some extent. Others simply find a different job and put the experience behind them when they leave. Yet some feel more impacted, psychologically or professionally, and to varying degrees. These are the people who, when compared to those who can just suck it up or leave, are sometimes seen as weak or having unrealistic expectations about how they deserve to be treated in the workplace. What is so different between these people or their situations that elicits these different reactions?

I believe that how people react has to do with their attachments or lack thereof. At least, that's what was true for me. I will explore the impact those attachments had on me, how they opened me up to the harassment and violence I experienced, and finally how I found my way out of it. The characters are real, but not their names.

ATTACHMENTS

SETTING IT UP

Fall 2014

I WAS 36 years old, married to a good man, and mother to a two-year-old daughter. I had a master's degree in social work, though I never practised in the field, as I chose to carve out a career in policy development: I preferred to create meaningful change for many people at one time over helping people one at a time, not that the latter wasn't important (it just wasn't "me"). I considered myself to be intelligent, self-sufficient, and cool under pressure. I had also run for political office twice (provincial in 2007 and municipal in 2010) and did volunteer work. I was – and still am – proud of who I was and what I had accomplished so far in life.

I was also three years into my first "career job." I loved it. I had had plenty of jobs before this one, some at the same agency as this one, but this was the first one in an area where I wanted a future for myself. The project I worked on, a survey that gathered information on numerous aspects of a person's life over time, had a purpose and potential that I greatly believed in. It also provided room to grow both in skills and in knowledge, which itself made many promotional opportunities possible. I felt energized and purposeful when I reported to work each day, driven by a mental list of things I needed to do. I was continuously learning on this job, with each year bringing a different set of challenges that I endeavoured to overcome. I was never bored. In the first three years, I had already been promoted twice and was poised for more. I felt very fortunate.

But the project also had its difficulties. Budget cuts affected its viability and ability to bring in much-needed human and operational resources. We struggled to meet deadlines, to hire permanent and experienced staff, and to resolve problems easily and efficiently. A lot of us worked above – and sometimes below – our paygrade to fill the staffing gaps and get things done. This variety of duties helped me learn more and maintained my enthusiasm, and also develop attachments to the people I worked with.

I liked my co-workers as friends. We enjoyed each other's company at work enough that we welcomed opportunities to socialize with each other outside of it. Of course, like within many teams, there were times when I was exasperated with one of them or one of them was exasperated with me. However, we always managed to put our differences aside, get the job done, and move on. We were all dedicated to the project, and I don't think I was the only one to whom this project felt like more than just a paycheque. This genuine liking of each other and pulling together when times got tough were what attached me to them and, I think, helped us bond. It felt like we were in the trenches together.

I also respected and admired the man who managed the

project and our team, whom I will call The Boss. He had a great sense of humour – sometimes witty and wry, and sometimes with jokes that made others groan – and was also a good teacher who gave valuable professional advice and was easy to get along with. He had us over at his house each Christmas and even once hosted a summer party for us at his cottage. I also found him to be facially expressive. I felt you could tell whether he was happy or unhappy, stressed or relaxed, pondering or tired. This is partly why I liked him so much: he didn't act like some omniscient, detached superior being who lorded over his serfs. He was *human*. He had a heart.

I also valued his wisdom. He was a very intelligent, experienced man who knew how to share with less experienced and knowledgeable people. He could explain the most complex concepts in the simplest ways, often drawing pictures to explain his points. I welcomed any chance I had to watch and listen as he taught, soaking up anything and everything I could. I always came out of those discussions feeling smarter than before.

I felt I could trust him. His candidness was unusual for a manager, and it warmed me to him even more. He would sometimes give his opinion on people he used to work with, processes we had to adopt, and his career ups and downs. He was always professional, but still spoke honestly and directly. And, when he said he would do something, he *did it*.

All of these characteristics together made him the *package*. He had the wisdom, professional success, and leadership style that I wanted to develop for myself. I looked up to him as someone to emulate. For that reason, it became important to me that he thought well of me.

It was to this project and these people that I felt attached.

They were my friends, people I was comfortable and enjoyed being with, and with whom I felt united in a common objective that spoke to what I had gone to school for and hoped to accomplish professionally. And all under the tutelage of someone whom I almost revered, whose intelligence and success I wanted to mirror. I both needed and wanted to be where I was, for the friendships I had and the future I wanted to develop.

SHIFTING

I EXCITEDLY REJOINED my team after a year-long assignment in another division. I had kept in touch with them while I was away because I missed their camaraderie and the project. I had also kept in touch with The Boss, whom I reached out to a few times for advice about whether I was getting the professional development I needed from my assignment. I began clashing with my assignment manager towards the end because I wasn't getting the knowledge or experience that he had promised me, and he didn't appreciate me challenging that.

I was happy that there were so many familiar and friendly faces when I returned, but there were also a few new ones. *Happy additions*, I thought, and wanted to get to know and bond with them just like I had with everyone else on the team. Two of them were Sam and Erica, in their late 20s and early 30s respectively, who joined the team as permanent members a few months before I returned. They seemed to already be well established within the team's camaraderie by the time I met them, and so I fully expected that my bonds with the pre-existing members would extend to these two.

The Boss had been promoted to a senior management position that he had been wanting for a long time. It was bittersweet. I was happy that he finally got the promotion, but sad that it meant I was going to lose him as my manager. But he was still going to run our team till a replacement could be found, likely in a few months, so I felt we both got something that way.

Another shift was my new position. Before I returned, The Boss called me to say that he was making me responsible for the content development stage of the project's third iteration. I was excited about this. It showed that The Boss thought I was skilled and responsible enough to be trusted to lead. I felt flattered, valued, and highly motivated to give the project my all. This new role, combined with my long service and the influx of new project members, made me feel like I was a senior member of the team.

The final shift was the third new person on the team: the Number 2. Before now, The Boss didn't have a proper second-in-command, someone who could manage the project's daily operations while he took care of all of the administration and stakeholder relationships. The Number 2 was brought in to fill that gap, and The Boss was very happy to have him on board. He was relieved to have someone take over the tasks that had prevented him from fully focusing on what he was supposed to.

This meant that I was now reporting to the Number 2. I was disappointed that I wouldn't have as many opportunities to meet The Boss and glean knowledge from him. I was also surprised. The Number 2 had been brought into the team months before my return, but The Boss never mentioned this change in the hierarchy when he spoke to me about what my responsibilities would be. However, he had been stretched for some time and, having been promoted with no one yet to replace him, it became more important than ever that he have someone who could take care of the project's operational aspects. I wanted The Boss to be able to move on and enjoy the promotion he had sought for so long. The best way I could support him was by embracing the Number 2. I trusted The Boss's judgment, so if he liked the Number 2, then so would I.

However, I quickly found out that my colleagues had a different opinion.

Erica approached me one day to say how upset she was that she hadn't been getting along with the Number 2. I was surprised because I hadn't heard about any interpersonal issues on the team, and it bothered me because it disrupted the happy, cohesive view I had of it. I saw a problem that needed to be fixed. In what became the first of a few conversations, I answered her complaints with suggestions of other ways that the Number 2's behaviour could be interpreted, or advice on how she could approach him to resolve their differences. I wanted to keep my advice as neutral as possible because I didn't know the Number 2's side of this. After a few of these conversations, however, Erica told me that her own efforts to work with him had failed, that any other suggestions would fail if she tried them, and that other people had issues with him as well, including her supervisor, Louise. This is why, Erica said, she came to me for advice: if Louise was also having problems with him, then she couldn't expect much help from her.

I stopped giving advice when Erica told me she was tired of her attempts failing and wasn't going to try to work things out with the Number 2 anymore. Instead, she would ask Louise to be the liaison between her and the Number 2 so she wouldn't have to deal with him directly. She was grateful to have Louise as a buffer. I believed Erica when she said that she had tried everything she could to have a good relationship with him, but I was disappointed that we couldn't achieve harmony.

I soon began having difficulties with the Number 2 myself. I started sensing from him what I call "authoritarian-lite": an attitude where, because of his rank and role on the team, he felt it was his right to give orders to the employees below him and expect to be followed without question. Yes, his place in the team hierarchy gave him this right, but it can be hard to accept when you have more knowledge and experience with the project. What also made this hard for me to accept was that The Boss had told me that I would be the lead on my part of the project, which I assumed meant that I had the power to make decisions, not be someone who followed orders like an automaton. Instead, my input was shut down, sometimes condescendingly, by someone who didn't have the background that I did yet somehow thought he knew better. When I pushed back, he would give a vague reason for his direction or simply say that it was what he wanted, without further explanation. I spent my days feeling frustrated and dismissed.

I tried to get along with him and find common ground, but it became harder over time. He became increasingly rigid and less congenial. I tried to approach him the same way I had advised Erica, but he didn't seem receptive. He wouldn't attempt to meet me partway. I learned from a friend on the team, Mark, that he was like this with Louise and a few others as well, mostly the women. Our team was a fifty/fifty male-female split, and all the females on the team had the same or similar problem with him as I did. Mark also told me that Louise once spoke to The Boss about him, only to be told that the Number 2 was here to stay and she had to learn to work with him.

In October, I became eligible for a promotion. A pool of candidates was going to be created for people who, like me, were deemed qualified. Any manager who needed someone at the higher level could pull someone from the pool, at which point the qualified person would be promoted. I was excited about the possibility, but I felt conflicted. I still loved the project, but the team I rejoined wasn't the one I had left for my assignment. It didn't have the camaraderie that I remembered so fondly; I felt stifled and I attributed it to the Number 2. I felt that as long as he was around and did his "authoritarian-lite," the joy of working on that team would slowly disappear and the experienced people would leave. I didn't want the team to fall apart because of one individual but, if The Boss wouldn't step in to resolve the problem, then there was little I could do. It felt as though the ship was about to sink and if I couldn't save it, then I had to save myself. Disloyal perhaps, but necessary.

I thought about my potential promotion. Oftentimes someone would be picked out of a pool by their own team, and it was assumed that The Boss would do that for me. It was equally assumed that I would accept that offer, as not many people switched teams when there was a ready promotion waiting for them in the current one. I wasn't obliged to accept, but it saddened me to leave something I felt passionately about. Then it occurred to me: could I use my eventual free agency to create a positive change?

Louise's failed attempt to address the issues with the Number 2 told me that any leveraging I'd attempt would fail. However, The Boss deserved to know that I was thinking of leaving and why. If he was willing to do something to encourage me to stay, great, but I felt that he would cut me loose. I told him that I had concerns with the team. He booked us a meeting in a private room where we sat at a large conference table, him on one side and me on the other. The width couldn't have been more than a couple of metres, but it felt like he was on the other side of the room.

I began by explaining the difficulties I was having trying to work with the Number 2 and how I didn't think I could make any headway with him. I finished by saying that if I was offered the promotion with the team today, I would reject it because I didn't want to work with the Number 2.

The Boss's reaction shook me. He rose from his seat and walked angrily to the door, saying, "If you want to go that badly, I won't stop you."

I immediately felt a sharp pain in my heart. I had expected him to say the proverbial "sorry it didn't work out," shake my hand, and wish me well in my job search. But no. The good man whom I looked up to and whose good opinion I valued now hated me. I was panicked because this was all happening so quickly and I feared that I had irreparably damaged my relationship with him. My head yelled at me, *Don't let him leave like this!*

As he put his hand on the doorknob, I turned to him and said, "Do you think this is easy for me?"

He paused and let go of the doorknob, his face softening. "No, I don't think it is," he said, returning to his seat.

We talked more about what had been happening. I told him that I valued and wanted to keep my position, but that the work relationship was strained to the point that I felt I had to make a choice. I said that I was told others had approached him about the Number 2 in the past only to be told that he supported the Number 2 and nothing would change. I offered to leave because I didn't want him to think I was asking him to choose between me and the Number 2. The Boss said he understood where I was coming from, but countered that leaving might work against me. "Managers," he continued, "might wonder why you're not being picked up by your own team. And your problems with the Number 2 show your tendency to have problems with your supervisors."

I immediately felt defensive. I knew he was talking about my assignment manager, and he was combining that with my problems with the Number 2 to conclude that the issue was with me and not with those who managed me.

"A manager might wonder if something was wrong with me for not staying with my team but, if anyone chose to look deeper, they would find a team where every female either left or was looking to leave and wonder why. If they trace it back to him, then I won't be the only one who'll look bad." I meant to simply defend myself, but later I realized that he might have interpreted it as a threat.

The Boss asked me if I would stay if he could fix what was happening. I said I would. So he agreed to intervene in exchange for me staying with the team. He said it in a way that felt apologetic, kind, and sincere. Knowing how much he liked the Number 2, I felt that his willingness to intervene was a compromise to keep us both. I felt supported and valued and wanted. And I swore to myself that, through hard work and dedication to the project, I would do my best to prove that he hadn't made a mistake.

Things were better for a while. The Boss attended any meetings that I had with the Number 2. The Boss's presence encouraged more productive conversations, and he made decisions about the project that fairly took both our points of view into account. It wasn't creating a better working relationship between myself and the Number 2, but at least we weren't butting heads anymore. It would have been better if the Number 2 and I had found some common ground and been able to work together without The Boss's intervention, whose involvement I felt some guilt over needing. But things had in fact improved, and so I considered the situation resolved.

DISSOLVING

2015

I FELT COMFORTABLE too soon.

After I returned from my Christmas holiday, I felt something had changed in how The Boss related to me and to the Number 2. They looked more "buddy-buddy" to me, like they had their own private clique. The Boss still played a neutral role in our meetings but, outside of them, he paid attention only to the Number 2. For example, he and I could be talking in the hall and, if he saw the Number 2 coming, he'd turn away from me while I was in mid-sentence to start talking to him. Or they would share an inside joke in front of me or leave together at the end of a meeting chatting while I was still gathering my things. He was like the teenage girl who dumps her friends the minute she sees her boyfriend walk down the hallway at school.

I thought at first that I was being overly sensitive. I told myself that there was nothing personal about this and he could be friends with whomever he wanted. He had a synergy with the Number 2 that he didn't have with me, and there was nothing wrong or unusual about that. But after a few weeks I started thinking that this *was* personal, suspecting that he resented me for what I had said to him in the fall and that he wanted to demonstrate that he liked the Number 2 a lot more than he liked me. All of this was just a gut feeling, though, till I noticed that my promotion wasn't happening as quickly as I thought it would. I entered the pool in the fall of 2014 but, a few months into 2015, there were still no papers. He never seemed concerned that Human Resources hadn't sent them. I asked him three times if he knew what was happening with them, to which each time he said he'd look into it and then didn't. And he'd respond rather nonchalantly, too, as if he didn't care whether those papers came or not. This went on for weeks. I didn't understand. Didn't he want to keep me? Didn't he want to make sure I maintained my end of our agreement?

At this point, most reasonable people would conclude that they weren't as valued as they thought, and that possibly The Boss wasn't as worthy of their loyalty and gratitude either. However, I had an attachment to him. He was the first person in authority whom I looked up to as a mentor, and I had promised myself to support him. I wanted him to think well of me and my potential at the agency. It didn't occur to me that he would ask me to stay for any reason other than that he valued me, but the exclusion and dismissiveness showed that my assumption had been wrong. And if I was wrong about that, then what other interactions between us – the teaching moments, the jokes, him asking me to stay – was I wrong about as well? I couldn't believe that I had misinterpreted so much. No, his opinion of me changed, and it was my fault.

But I was still angry at how he so clearly favoured someone who had alienated literally half the team, including people who had admired and respected him long before Number 2 showed up. It felt like a betrayal. But I had a good history with him and so I couldn't accept that his favouritism was intentional. I repeatedly told myself that The Boss would change if he knew how his behaviours were being interpreted. And if it had been me in the Number 2's position, challenged by half of the team, then I might need and appreciate having the very support that The Boss was showing him. So, I tried to let go of my insecurities and keep my expectations in check. The best thing I could do was to remain committed to being the employee The Boss could trust and rely on, so that one day he would again value my contributions.

But as much as I told myself this and kept plowing through my work, the insecurities about favouritism and resentment didn't go away. I started waking up between 4:30 and 5 o'clock in the morning, trying to make sense of it all.

These early wake-ups signalled the beginning of my slowly deteriorating mental health.

I think a lot of people have conversations in their head with other people, especially if they're trying to resolve something with them. You imagine how you would start the conversation, how that person might respond, then how you'd respond, and so on. Personally, I think it can be an effective way to prepare yourself for difficult conversations.

But I couldn't control mine. My brain would just turn on in the early-morning hours and start racing. It would take what I saw from the days and weeks before and speculate about what it meant, multiple hypotheses darting out simultaneously. My brain would latch on to one and imagine the different ways I should deal with it, including what I could say to The Boss to resolve it. I went through this exercise daily, *involuntarily*, with another day's observations added to the next morning's ruminations.

And each day, I'd eventually become aware that I shouldn't stay in bed immersed in these thoughts. I would tell myself, *Get up. Stop lying in bed thinking about this.* But I couldn't. My brain felt compelled to finish whatever train of thought I ended up on, however long and through however many different scenarios it took me. And even though I knew that these were just speculations being driven by my imagination, I couldn't counteract them because there was no evidence that what I was imagining *couldn't* be real. And so the early wake-ups continued, me trying to sort out imagination from reality.

I needed to do something to calm my brain.

In March, I decided that I needed to ask The Boss if he knew how the Number 2 felt about working with me. His intervention, though helpful, couldn't be long-term. The Number 2 and I needed to figure out how to work together without The Boss, but neither of us had spoken since the intervention started so I felt uneasy initiating that conversation. But even more important was my need to counteract my imaginings. A friendly conversation with him could do that.

When we met, I explained that not much had changed between the Number 2 and me, but that I wondered if there was anything he knew that might improve it. The Boss answered that a change was coming – and later that week he announced that the Number 2 was leaving at the end of April for a position in another agency. *Okay*, I told myself. *It's dif-*

ficult now, but everything will go back to how it used to be. The Boss will see your value again. Just be patient.

The early wake-ups still continued, but I told myself that all my insecurities would end soon.

In April, The Boss announced that the team would be getting a new manager, Laura. She was experienced and would take over the team gradually while transitioning out of her current position, with him staying involved till that was complete.

I also received, and signed, my promotion papers, but my relief was mingled with disappointment over The Boss's seeming disinterest in it, having done nothing to expedite them and by having the division's administrative assistant give them to me instead of presenting them himself. Despite that, signing them showed that I kept my promise to stay if he helped resolve the situation with the Number 2.

We finished developing the survey's content in May and now I was knee-deep in the next stage: developing and testing the project's data-gathering application. It was important for us to get this right because we used this application to collect and send back the answers people gave us to our questions. Any mistakes could mean incomplete or wrong information. However, we were also on a tight deadline, and this stage had been hindered by problems and delays in the past. Producing a good quality application on time would have made The Boss happy and shown him that I could lead. We were nearly two months shy of our first deadline.

I was responsible for the first two development stages and Louise for the last two. She also played a quality-check role in mine, so being successful depended a lot on us being able to work together. Unfortunately, she was dealing with what I now believe was depression. It wasn't something I fully understood at the time, and she might not have either. This, plus the lack of a structured plan to address it, led to professional and interpersonal issues between us.

Louise's depression led to sporadic and unpredictable absences from the office. It also impacted her ability to complete work on time, causing me to fall behind on my deliverables because I had been waiting for her to finish her quality checks. Every few days, I'd follow up with her and she'd promise to finish a certain number of them, but then wouldn't or only some of them. She was adamant that I wait for her, saying her input was essential.

I resented her unreliability and unwillingness to prioritize them. Some days, instead of working on what she knew I needed from her, she'd let herself into my office and vent about things in her personal life that were bothering her. I appreciated that she saw me as someone she could lean on, but I'd be thinking about every quality check I was waiting on from her. I grew increasingly anxious about being able to finish the first stage on time.

One day, I lost all patience. During a meeting to acquaint Laura with the project, I made a split-second decision to ask Louise, in front of both Laura and The Boss, when I could expect the overdue quality checks. I looked ugly for sure, but I was too frustrated and stressed to care and felt this would pressure her to get them done. She finished all the outstanding checks the next day and a lot of my stress dissipated, but she later told me how upset and disappointed she was that I hadn't come to her first with my concerns. I restrained myself from reminding her about the numerous times I *had* asked, and just walked away.

It was during this time that Erica started venting to me about similar frustrations with Louise. I was taken aback because it was only a couple of months earlier when she had told me how grateful she was to have Louise as a buffer between her and the Number 2. But within a couple of months after the Number 2 left, Erica started making cutting and non-empathetic remarks about her to me. Some were accurate but I still felt dismayed by how quickly she turned on Louise after saying she was grateful to have her as that buffer. I didn't comment on any of them because she intimidated me.

Erica and I became friends over our experiences with the Number 2 and I found her fun to be around. However, when she had a negative opinion about someone or something, she'd express it bitingly, with a sharpness, quickness, and strength that tightened my chest. If you disagreed, then she'd tell you that you weren't seeing things clearly, and so definitively as to shut down the conversation. I knew her public venting was mean and inappropriate but, between the stress of the development, the emotional impact of The Boss's favouritism, and the sleepless nights, I didn't have the psychological energy to confront her nor the clarity to know how. I told myself that as long as Louise wasn't hearing it, then no great harm was being done.

My impatient brain kept waking early, wondering how I could rebuild my relationship with The Boss now that the Number 2 was gone. I had to be helpful, intelligent, and professional, and not appear paranoid or needy (which I thought I was being). Since he was a researcher, I thought of proposing a research activity that could help the project. And why wouldn't I be the lead of my own idea?

I was stunned when he suggested it would be a good project for Sam.

It took me a moment to recover, saying meekly, "I think Sam is busy with his work. I don't think he has the time."

"There isn't anyone else who can do this," he said. "*He* could have, but he's gone now," referring to the Number 2. He then sighed and resumed his work.

I'm here, I thought. *I can do it.* My head was screaming at me to say those words, stand up for myself, remind him of my capabilities, but I was too surprised, hurt, and tired to do so. I also feared hearing that he didn't think I was capable. And so I left his office, timidly thanking him for his time.

My 4:30 a.m. wake-ups continued. My insecurities kept popping up in my head, strengthened by this rejection. I tried to convince myself that I was being unreasonable. *Of course he wouldn't ask you to lead a research activity*, I told myself. *You're busy managing the development. He needs you to focus on that.* I told myself that the early wake-ups were from the stress of managing the project.

The first development stage ended well and on time. I had buried myself in it to make that happen, by necessity as much as by choice. The busyness also kept me from thinking about The Boss or the doubts and hurt I felt, but what I didn't deal with during the day continued to demand an audience each day before dawn.

I kept my family out of this as much as possible. I wanted as much separation between my work and home life as I could get, and I didn't have the mental or emotional energy to explain the work environment and my colleagues to them. So, as soon as I'd get home, I'd immediately head to the daycare to pick up my daughter and spend the rest of my day focusing on her needs till she went to bed.

But I did unload during the daily lunchtime walks with my friend and fellow team member Mark – even sometimes during our occasional nights out at the pub. It wasn't fair to use him as a sounding board for all of this, but I had no one else and he knew who and what I'd be talking about. He had a very different opinion of The Boss. He simply considered him a bad manager and saw no grey area for a positive interpretation of The Boss's choices. Mark thought The Boss played favourites and was coldly detached from everyone else. He couldn't understand why I was conflicted about a manager who never spared a thought towards me and would quickly forget me if I quit. He told me this every time I defended The Boss and was frustrated with me for not seeing him as clearly as he did.

To me, however, Mark was unforgiving and unempathetic. I recognized and valued a history with The Boss that Mark seemed to dismiss. Mark was black and white, starkly angry and dark, where I saw grey and wanted to have hope.

It was summer now. We were well set up for stage two. And my 4:30 a.m. wake-ups became 4 a.m. wake-ups.

Louise was still working through her depression and I was still her sometimes-counsellor. She told me that she didn't like her role on the team and started applying for jobs elsewhere, but then she'd change her mind, again and again for several weeks. I'd occasionally ask what her plans were because I suspected a lot of her responsibilities would come to me if she left, but then I asked one too many times.

"Stop asking me about it," she yelled. "It's obvious you want me to leave and you're trying to push me out! Why *else* would you keep asking about my job search?"

She wasn't completely wrong. I wasn't trying to push her out, but she was obviously unhappy and I felt she needed to leave. We barely spoke after her outburst, and I resigned myself to being uncertain about what my responsibilities might be in a few months.

Erica and I started socializing together outside of work. She had become a confidante regarding my issues with The Boss, Louise, and my early mornings. She knew a lot about my mental state, and I continued to hear her complain about Louise, her comments becoming even more biting.

My unresolved insecurities about The Boss continued to take a toll on me. I caught up on sleep on Saturdays only every couple of months, crashing on the couch for a few hours after breakfast. There was no reprieve outside of that. I knew I had to clear the air with him about the resentment and devaluation I felt, and I felt that having kept the project running smoothly and on schedule merited me an audience.

Yet, despite this confidence, it took me a while to build the courage to approach him. I felt that raising these insecurities was akin to bringing him a problem to fix, breaking my promise to be supportive. That rang through my head when I finally did find the courage to walk up to his door, but only to stand paralyzed outside of it, unable to bring myself to knock. I tried again a few days later. As I stood frozen at his door again, debating whether I really wanted to do this, he walked up behind me and said hello. The decision had been made for me: I had to go in.

He sat at his desk and I sat facing him, probably no more

than a couple of metres away but feeling much further. I felt anxious. I had to start talking. "I know you don't think much about these things –"

"You're right. I don't."

I froze. The quick, dismissive interruption made me lose my nerve. I quickly started some small talk to give myself time to regroup. I broached the topic again, letting it trail off with "but if you don't think about these things ..."

I hoped he would cut in and tell me to continue, but he remained silent, staring at me, almost coldly. I understood that to mean he didn't want to hear what I wanted to say, so I thanked him for his time and left, cowed, defeated. He was not going to help me: I would have to figure out on my own which insecurities were real and which were imagined.

The 4 a.m. wake-ups continued, followed by thoughts of trying to reconcile the kind, wise mentor with the cold and detached man I'd met with. *He wouldn't have turned me away if he knew what was going through my head*, I told myself. *He's too busy managing his new role while still leading the team.* I was too attached to who he *was* that I couldn't shift my thinking to see him for who he became.

I spent the early-morning hours processing these thoughts about him, my days pushing through the project, but evenings were focused on my daughter. I continued to tell myself that my work responsibilities were causing my stress and sleepless mornings, and that my issues with The Boss were simply a symptom. In the meantime, Laura told me that she needed me to take on the last two development stages that Louise was supposed to be responsible for so she could complete other priorities she'd fallen behind on.

One day in July, I found myself with two tickets to a professional soccer game that I couldn't attend. I knew that Sam's wife was a fan, so I offered them to him. He gladly accepted and gave me a bottle of wine as thanks. I didn't think we were allowed alcohol in the workplace, so I looked at that bottle in my bottom cabinet drawer with a bit of gleeful rebelliousness, though I was anxious to get it home before someone saw me with it. However, as I continued looking at it, I thought of how often I'd heard of people succumbing to alcoholism while trying to cope with difficult life problems. *Well, I can't drink my problems away*, I thought. *I'd lose my job.* And I joked with myself that I would never deteriorate to using drugs or gambling as coping behaviours, the way some people did, because I couldn't afford it!

Then, if I want to escape this, I thought, *I'd have to kill myself.*

I knew immediately how wrong and dark this was, but not so wrong or dark that I shouldn't entertain it. I thought of my daughter. Could I leave her? *Yes*, I thought. In fact, I concluded she'd be better off without me and is young enough that she wouldn't remember me. If I really want to do this, I'd have to do it now.

But how? *First*, I thought, *it would have to look like an accident.* I have a young daughter at home and she can't grow up knowing that her mother chose to leave her. So, no shooting, hanging, or cutting myself. What would look like an accident? *I could get hit by a car*, I thought, *but I'd have to look like I wasn't paying attention crossing the street.* Fine, but some people survive getting hit by cars, and "only" end up with serious and painful injuries. I didn't want that. I wanted a quick and certain death.

So it'd have to be by a truck. I then started wondering how often I'd seen big trucks along the road by my office. Conclusion: just often enough to make this idea possible.

But was success guaranteed? Would it be certain that it'd look like an accident and that death would be immediate? I wasn't sure. I also thought of the truck driver and felt guilty for the horrible memory my action would cause.

So, after about a month of this to-and-fro in my head, I dropped the idea. Not because of any new-found sense of hope or desire to live, but because I couldn't accomplish it for sure the way I wanted to. I'd simply resigned myself to living the life I had.

Despite how dark these thoughts were, I never saw them as anything I needed to address. I still showed up to work every day, did my work well and on time, picked up my daughter from daycare daily, and took care of all her needs. I still showered, dressed well, and kept the house relatively clean. I didn't have any of the outward signs that something was terribly wrong, so I therefore had to be okay. These thoughts were done with and, I told myself, *I'm fine now*.

I was in denial about myself during this time, but I clearly saw what was going on with Sam. Mark and I recognized that he was struggling. He had tasks that needed to be done perfectly, but no experience doing them, and so his learning curve was steep. However, Sam would never admit that he needed help. He came to work every day without fail and plugged through his work as hard as he could. Unlike me, it really *was* the work that was causing his stress. He had been doing the job of two or three people for months. He seemed to be cracking, but if you asked him how he was, he would slap on a smile and cheerily say he was fine. His eyes answered differently.

He was a sweet, intelligent, and talented man with a bright future ahead of him. Mark and I liked him and wanted to see him succeed, so we took it upon ourselves to get him out of the office over as many lunch hours as we could. We would walk outside, talking about whatever interested us at the moment. It wasn't therapy per se, but it was a break from the job. I believe it gave Sam a mental reset that helped carry him through the rest of the day.

Eventually, he started talking about the pressures he was facing, not in great detail nor with any show of distress, but enough to demonstrate his feelings. In turn, I shared the pressures I had been feeling from the deadlines and challenges I was dealing with in development. I joked about bringing in a box full of china that we could spend a lunch hour throwing against a wall somewhere. He chuckled softly at the idea. I hoped it told him that he wasn't alone, that there were other very capable people nearby who were struggling too. I wanted him to feel validated and understood, and to know that he didn't have to bottle up his feelings.

Our conversations stayed between Sam, Mark, and me because I felt that if I ever broke his confidence and tried to seek help for him, he would stop talking altogether. I debated throughout the summer whether I should approach management, knowing I would risk losing his trust. We continued these walks and conversations privately and, over time, Sam became a friend.

In late summer, The Boss met with Louise, Laura, and me to announce that Laura would soon take over his responsibilities full-time. I felt surprised because the transition had been going on for so long that I had gotten used to the status quo. After the meeting, The Boss asked me to go with him for coffee in the cafeteria. I agreed and wondered if this was my chance to raise some of the questions I was struggling to answer.

But I didn't know how. We found a table in the back and I opened the conversation by asking about the rules surrounding mental health leaves, as I had an employee who had recently left on one. I felt that could lay the groundwork for raising my insecurities and perceptions. Instead, thinking about my own mental state while hearing him talk about leaves triggered all the pent-up emotions that I had been dealing with. I started tearing up, so I placed my hands on my cheeks in a weak effort to hide them, to pull myself together.

He kept talking, almost non-stop, barely looking at me the whole time. I wanted to explain why I looked so upset, but I froze. I screamed in my head to interrupt him and tell him what had been going on, but the words wouldn't come out. I don't remember how long we were there or how the meeting ended, but I had recovered by the time we walked out of the cafeteria to return to our floor.

We were the only ones in the elevator, standing at the back in opposite corners. As soon as the doors closed, he slumped slightly, brought a hand to his forehead, and sighed heavily. Relief from our coffee meeting finally being over? Exasperation from seeing me become emotional? It could have been about something completely unrelated, but my gut said that it was about me. My heart sank. He darted off the elevator as soon as the doors opened, before I could even take a step. This incident added even more to the early-morning work of trying to reconcile observation with reason.

Come September, I became less concerned about breaking

Sam's confidence than getting him help. He was getting darker, more hopeless. I was worried about him eventually doing something harmful if no one ever intervened in a meaningful way. He needed someone to take over part of his workload. I told Laura about it and she asked him, discreetly, how everything was and he'd said that everything was fine. Laura told me that she still took what I'd said seriously and bring in someone to help, which I was grateful for. She hired a skilled, intelligent person to help Sam for a year. Sam became an unofficial supervisor of the new team member's work, which was a great development experience for him. I could see his stress fading. Dealing with Sam, my anxiety around Louise, and my heavy workload helped me ignore the psychological impact of my own problems: I was now waking up at 3:30 in the morning.

I expected that the transition at work would mean that I would start interacting more with Laura and be able to detach from The Boss. This was mostly the case but once in a while he would reinsert himself to ask me to do something. He had the right of course since he was The (Top) Boss, but I found it hard to detach when he'd drop me, come back when he wanted something, then drop me again. I resented that he wouldn't have the difficult conversations with me yet still expected me to act cheerfully and obey his orders gladly. I responded by putting as much distance between us as I could. No office visits, no eye contact in meetings, no initiated conversations. Creating distance meant cutting him out.

This came to a head in the fall when The Boss asked me to make changes late in the development. I was frustrated as I knew our programmers wouldn't appreciate redoing work already signed off on, and I feared the changes would cause a delay. A colleague made a joke about it and I snapped at him for it. Loudly.

Suddenly, all of my unresolved issues from the year bubbled over. Think of it as trying to clean the dining car of an old steam train only to be told, before you're done, that another dining car must get cleaned immediately. You bring the dishes from its tables to the kitchen for washing, but leave them piled there, still dirty, because you need to tidy the next car. Then, once the next car's dishes are piled in the kitchen, you need to go tidy yet another dining car. In short, you're doing just enough to make the car look pretty, but you haven't done the work to clean and put things away. This is how it was with The Boss and Louise: I never dealt with how I resented them for the stress and anger they caused me. I had no unresolved feelings toward Sam, but I was trying to help him clean *his* dishes instead of my own, which piled high and came crashing down.

The colleague I snapped at had been friendly with me for years, so I felt he would know that I was just venting. But Laura admonished me for my comments and told me to keep a lid on my frustrations in the future. The Boss also found out about it and summoned me to a private meeting to remind me that it was his right to make changes when he wanted to and it was my responsibility to implement them. He also said he'd noticed I had become prickly and standoffish with him in recent months, and he didn't know why.

This time, through my anger at his hypocrisy, and possibly the distance I had created between us, emboldened me to stand up for myself. Instead of just taking the criticism and leaving as I had before, I told him that I was frustrated with him for rejecting my attempts to discuss issues I had with him. He answered that he didn't realize I had issues, but now that he knew, we should meet again to hash this out once and for all.

I was proud of myself for speaking up and relieved that I'd get the opportunity to address the insecurities and issues I'd been dealing with since January. I worried though that he would forget about the request or change his mind about discussing it, so I booked a meeting for us in two weeks' time, adding a note in the invitation for him to accept only if he was still willing to have this conversation. I waited. Then the day before the meeting was to take place, he rejected the invitation, writing that any problems I have should be discussed with Laura. That was it.

I had told him straight to his face that the issues were directly related to him, and he passed me on to someone else. I was hurt. I could no longer tell myself that he'd have acted differently if he knew what had been going on. I was done with him now.

It was now November. Development ended and I went on a two-week holiday to get away from the stress. I expected to return to work fully rested and back to my normal self. I didn't. My 3:30 a.m. wake-ups continued.

SHARKS

CIRCLING

2016

WE WERE A month into the next phase of the project, data collection. I was managing it because Louise was leaving in a month for a new position. I didn't want the job because I had hoped to get into more analytical work instead, but I knew I had the rank and experience to fill the role. It was a relief to see Louise move on, but as much for her sake as mine. I hoped a role change would help her find joy in work again.

My walks with Sam became less frequent. I was disappointed because I considered him a friend and enjoyed our conversations, but relieved that his mental health seemed much better than before. The employee whom Laura had brought in to support him was very useful and Sam flourished in his new guiding role. He also got promoted to the same level as me, which he fully deserved.

Sam was also receiving accolades for a paper he wrote about the project, so much so that he was asked to present it at an international symposium being held locally. It was easy to see the joy and pride on his face and I was happy for him. It was if all the stress and pressure he experienced in the last year was now paying itself off. A bright future was lining up for him.

Erica continued to work under me and I officially became her supervisor once Louise left. She was very experienced with data collection and I could trust her to handle the daily ins and outs of the project while I handled the more complex issues that arose. I saw her as my own second-in-command, and even told her that I thought she had the potential to move up.

Our friendship also continued. We commiserated over our lives and she gave her opinions in her direct, no-nonsense way. I believed she really wanted to help, but she could still sound mean, unapologetic in her opinions and dismissive of alternative points of view. I felt disagreeing with her would be useless, and it wasn't important to me if she agreed with me.

We also welcomed a new team member, Helen. Laura hired her as a second-in-command (her own Number 2) to help manage the team's daily operations. My same-level colleague, Mylène, and I were now reporting to Helen.

I had a good first impression of her. She had experience leading projects similar to ours and would share what she could to help us, but said that she wouldn't hesitate to ask us for help on anything that she didn't know about, which I liked. She was the opposite of the Number 2. I felt she would fit better with the team than he had.

I found her to be honest, straightforward, and easy to get along with. I was her employee, but felt treated like a colleague. And because she wasn't afraid to appear fallible with me, I wasn't afraid to appear fallible with her. I felt comfortable with her.

I also appreciated the genuine interest she showed in

team members' lives. If someone had a dilemma or was going through a difficult time, Helen would listen attentively, reacting to the twists and turns of the story, and provide empathetic comments and advice. She wanted to be everyone's friend as well as their boss.

So, over the first few months of 2016, my work life quieted down, but I still kept waking up at 3:30 a.m. to ruminate over the past year. I was forced to acknowledge that my workload and deadlines weren't the cause of my sleeplessness.

I saw my doctor in March. He immediately put me on a wait-list for assessment at a hospital sleep clinic, but suggested I try melatonin in the meantime. He also referred me to a psychologist experienced in sleep issues. I knew sleep problems could be caused by underlying psychological issues, but I didn't feel that I needed that kind of help. I was the one with the social work degree; I was the helper, not the one who needed help. I believed that medication, not therapy, would get my sleeping back on track.

I tried the melatonin for two weeks. No effect. The doctor suggested I try non-prescription antihistamines to induce sleep, but they worked only one night. And the non-prescription sleeping pills you can buy off the shelf stopped working after a few nights.

Then the doctor prescribed sleeping pills, and those *did* work. I slept longer than I had in a year. But I knew they could be addictive, so I chose to take a pill only every other night. I quickly learned that wouldn't work: on the nights when I didn't take a pill, I'd wake up between 1 and 2 a.m., as if my brain felt it needed to perversely compensate for the extra sleep it got the night before. Waking at 3:30 a.m. was difficult enough, but even *earlier* both physically and psychologically crushed me. I returned the unused pills to the pharmacy, even though the wait-list I was on was nearly a year long. My new normal was sleepless nights and waiting for the clinic to call.

But I still needed an outlet for all the stress and disappointment that I carried from the past year. I'd taken on a lot in handling my workload, trying to support Sam, managing my working relationship with Louise, and working through everything that went wrong with The Boss. It remained with me because I never acknowledged – it never *occurred* to me to acknowledge – the psychological weight of it all. Wanting and trying to be supportive, a friend, a quality employee, manager material, *good enough*, took a lot of psychological energy from me. But the stressors had accumulated so gradually that it took some time for me to feel their impact.

Instead, I saw others' stress and their difficulties in managing it, as well as how talking openly about it was something that earned contempt instead of support. Louise continued to be denigrated by Erica months after she left, joined by Helen and Isaac who took over a file of hers. Sam still denied feeling stress. This team didn't respect those who made mistakes or spoke openly about their mental health struggles. Such people were seen as weak, and so I decided to keep my mouth shut.

What helped open my eyes was our move to an open office environment – no more cubicles. We moved from an illusion of privacy to four people sharing a rectangular space, each with a desk in a corner of it, and walls around the border that were still low enough to see over them when you were seated. Everything and everyone were around you all the time. It was no longer easy to ignore behaviours or comments that were happening right next to you, and no one could pretend that their conversations were private.

I shared my space with Erica, Helen, and Isaac: I had a window seat in one corner, with Erica sitting roughly two metres behind me, facing the corridor, while Helen had the window seat in the other corner with Isaac in the corridor-facing seat behind her. Erica and Helen would regularly talk out loud and within earshot of nearby colleagues, including when it was about people who weren't there to defend themselves (like Louise).

I saw a problem. The unchecked denial and insults could worsen if the right conditions presented themselves, and spread wider because of the open environment. I also began to feel isolated by the silence that I felt I needed to keep to protect myself from the negativity around me. So, to help myself and the team, I signed up for a mental health workshop to see if there was something I could do to help us. I spoke with the facilitator about what I was witnessing and asked for advice on how to address it. She suggested that the team create a code of conduct: a document that describes what is acceptable and unacceptable behaviour, how unacceptable behaviour or other difficulties would be addressed, and the role of each working level of the team in monitoring and enforcing it. I thought this idea could work.

I called a meeting with Helen, Mylène, and Sam to propose it. I explained how I believed some of us on the team had experienced challenges last year with workload and mental health, and I was concerned about the negative comments I had heard about those who faced some of these challenges. Unchecked, they could lead to issues within the team. Creating a code of conduct could address the behaviours we saw now and prevent issues from occurring.

Helen and Sam didn't support the idea. Helen said we didn't need it because last year's problems were over and, in her opinion, wouldn't repeat. I pushed back, saying that we couldn't know whether or not they would repeat, and that now was a good time to work on it since we were in a much better position mentally. "Better now than wait till there's a problem," I said.

Sam said, somewhat condescendingly, "I don't need a piece a piece of paper to tell me how to behave."

But Mylène supported the idea. She too was concerned about mental health at work, though for different reasons, and she thought working to make the environment healthier was a good thing to do. Her support encouraged Helen to compromise: no code of conduct, but she would talk to Laura about holding mental health training for the team. I felt that this was the best I was going to get.

I was disappointed, and a bit surprised, by the strength of Sam's refusal and Helen's dismissiveness, especially since she was contributing to them with her own badmouthing. Her and Sam's resistance left me wondering whether improvement was actually possible.

The code of conduct idea wasn't the only thing I got out of that workshop. I also learned about the mental health continuum: a grid of four differently coloured columns – green, yellow, orange, red – matched against four rows that indicate where signs of a mental health issue can be seen – changes in mood, thinking and attitude, behaviour and performance, and physical state. The colours represented how someone would behave if they were mentally well (green), all the way to someone who was ill (red), with reacting (yellow) and injured (orange) in between. I stared at the grid, impressed by its clarity. *Everyone should see this*, I thought. Then I looked more closely at the behaviours it mentioned. What I saw hit me like a brick. The thoughts, feelings, and changes I had experienced over the last year, some of which were still plaguing me now, were all under orange and red. My mood ("recurrent, intrusive thoughts") and thinking and attitude ("anger" and "anxiety") were in the orange, while my physical state ("can't fall asleep or stay asleep") and play thoughts about killing myself were in the red (I still thought I was green for behaviour and performance).

Seeing so clearly just how severe my symptoms were forced me to acknowledge how unwell I was.

Data collection ended in June and we were now looking at what we got back. That's when I noticed a shift in Erica's behaviour. Seemingly overnight, her friendly tone turned cold and snarky. A *good morning* would be met with barely a glance at me and a cold hello. She openly questioned my direction, criticized my personal choices, and made otherwise judgmental comments about almost everything, well beyond the abrupt opinions I was used to. They were direct attacks, loud enough to be overheard by nearby co-workers.

Confused, I thought back to conversations, events, and decisions from recent weeks to see if there was something that could explain it. Nothing. I kept quiet for a while to see if this was temporary. Perhaps there was something happening in her personal life that was distressing her and, though inappropriate, she was lashing out as a way of dealing with it. But Erica only became harsher and her comments more frequent. After two weeks, I scheduled a meeting for us to talk, confident that a friendly conversation would clear everything up and we'd be able to resolve it. When the meeting time came, I explained that I had noticed her questioning my directions and choices, then asked, "Do you trust me?"

She looked directly at me and unhesitatingly replied, "No."

Then, without skipping a beat, she listed a slew of complaints about me, including every decision I'd made that she thought was wrong. She accused me of not listening to her. She spoke quickly, tersely, and without pause. It felt like a strong, sudden wind gust blew me straight into the back of my chair. All I could do was sit there, jaw gaping open at the verbal onslaught, trying to keep up mentally with the speed of her accusations while failing to remember the few that I could understand.

I was shocked and hurt. I wondered how to respond, but I didn't know how to confront all the examples she gave, so I focused instead on her claim that I didn't listen to her. I couldn't think of examples when I had ignored her or hadn't acknowledged her contributions, and I knew that I gave her my attention whenever she spoke to me. *What wasn't I getting?* I asked her to give me an example, to which she mentioned a decision I'd made several months earlier in development that she disagreed with. I said that I listened to her, I just didn't agree with her and, as the lead, it was my decision to make. "Well, you were still wrong," she replied, "and you should've known that."

I didn't know how to deal with this attitude, but I knew that being a supervisor meant being the bigger person. I told her I would listen better in the future. In return, I asked her to come to me sooner if she was unhappy so we could prevent situations like this from happening again. She agreed, then told me not speak to her in the mornings because she wasn't a morning person and didn't like socializing with people when she first arrived. I didn't believe her because I'd seen her chat with other people nearly every morning, but being the bigger person meant obliging her. I ended our meeting by telling her that I wanted us to meet again in two weeks to discuss our progress.

Of course, the very next day I saw her happily socializing with others in the morning. I continued respecting her request, though, and tried to speak with her later in the mornings and afternoons. Her comments were less snarky, but I could still hear the attitude behind them. She remained terse, strained, and cold. I tried to be a better listener, but she wasn't giving me much to listen to.

Our meeting at the two-week mark proved fruitless. She told me I hadn't changed enough and that I had misunderstood what she'd said about not listening to her. I was better prepared mentally for her this time and repeated the words she'd said at our last meeting, then asked her what I had misinterpreted. She denied saying those words, which she said proved her point, then, when I asked her to clarify what she meant, said nearly the exact sentence she had two weeks before. When I pointed that out, she answered, "You still don't get it." I asked for another example of what she meant, to which she said that she'd given me all of the examples in our last meeting and, for anything from the past two weeks, I should already know what those examples were.

The meeting ended worse than it began. The only good that came out of it was being allowed to speak to her in the mornings again, though this was only after I pointed out that others might think it odd that she was speaking to everyone but me. But around her, I felt confused, lost, and on edge. I was confused because I couldn't remember most of the decisions or conversations that Erica claimed had led to this and, for the few that I did, I couldn't understand how they had led to such contention. Lost because I didn't know how to resolve this without Erica's cooperation. And on edge because I had no idea how to communicate with or around her. I felt wary of saying anything to her because I didn't want to deal with her biting retorts.

I also didn't want to give her the opportunity to make more complaints about me. One day I opened a new hand moisturizer at my desk to find the scent being much stronger than I thought it would be. She turned around and snapped, "The smell is making me *choke*."

I was taken aback, as I had never known her to be sensitive to scents. The tone in her voice made it seem as though she was accusing me of intentionally trying to choke her. I cautiously replied, "I wasn't trying to make you choke."

"You should know better about how some people are sensitive to scents and not bring them into the workplace. You should be more considerate of those around you."

She then pulled out a fan, slammed it on the edge of her desk, pointed it towards me, and turned it on full blast. She then sharply turned back around in her chair and went back to work. I sat there, dumbfounded, shocked at her aggression and abruptness.

I had every right to discuss with her how she handled this situation, but I felt too nervous around her by now. *What sets her off? How should I respond to her attacks?* Not having slept well in months had taken its toll on my ability to think and react quickly, and made me distrust my memory: was I unable to remember the incidents Erica listed because they never happened or because I was too tired to think straight? Ultimately, I let it slide because I didn't have the psychological fortitude to be assertive with her.

It all came to a head in July when Helen got involved. Erica was again openly contradicting me in our workspace, this time about a work direction I gave that she bitingly disagreed with. Helen overheard and asked what was happening. I explained what we were disagreeing about, immediately after which Erica's angry stare turned into beseeching eyes and she said, quietly and almost sadly, "I just wish you would listen to me and try to understand where I'm coming from."

You two-faced witch, I thought.

I wasn't surprised that Erica would try to make me look bad to someone higher up – she had no trouble doing so publicly about others behind their backs – but I was shocked by how quickly and easily she turned herself into a misunderstood wounded party for my supervisor to see. Helen immediately came to Erica's defence, asking me why I wouldn't consider Erica's suggestions. I became defensive, feeling that I was now arguing with two people instead of one – and I did so while sitting with my back to my desk, facing Erica sitting at hers with Helen standing next to her almost in front of the only exit out of our workspace. I was literally cornered.

I felt angry and knew that the wise thing to do would be to leave the area so I could detach and calm down. I told them that I needed to go for a quick walk to clear my head. "So you're running away," Erica said. Helen silently looked at Erica, then back at me, as though she agreed with her. Now I was cornered *and* confined. I conceded to Erica's suggestions just so I could get out of the situation, in effect devaluing my role as the lead and rewarding her victim act and insubordination. And I was angry at Helen for taking a side in something that she didn't understand, and for not supporting my role as lead and supervisor. Publicly, too.

After things settled down, Helen met with me to apologize for upsetting me and to ask what was going on. She sounded like she wanted to help, which softened my anger. I explained, "I've been having a hard time with Erica over the last month. What you saw was just the most recent incident. As for how you intervened, please don't take it personally. You were simply collateral damage." This seemed to put Helen at ease. She asked if I needed guidance or support in dealing with Erica. I answered, "Thank you, but no. I don't want to involve anyone else right now and I'd like to resolve this myself. But, if I need help, I will let you know." Helen seemed satisfied with that. She said she would ask Erica for her side of the story as well.

I left that meeting feeling relieved: someone else now knew about what was going on, and that someone was in a position to support me. Even though I didn't immediately accept her help, I felt better knowing it was there if I needed it.

I started adding notes about my relationship progress with Erica in my weekly work-update emails to Helen. Unfortunately, there was never much new to write. No matter what I did or said, it seemed Erica was determined to hate me and make my life difficult. Erica's demonstrated willingness to deceive, combined with her insubordination and attacks, destroyed the trust I once had in her. The right time for me to assert myself as the supervisor was long past, but I still had to do it. And after the two-facedness she had shown with Helen, I felt no conflicting feelings in doing so.

I was taught that one of a supervisor's roles is to support their staff. That means giving them the training and guidance they need to do their jobs well, supporting their learning and development goals, and coaching them to make good corporate decisions. I hoped to get this from Helen when the time came to ask for it. Instead, I grew nervous. Soon after Helen and I spoke, and after she would have spoken to Erica about the dust-up in our workspace, I noticed the two of them socializing together more. Every few days or so, Erica would go to Helen's desk and ask if she wanted to join her in the cafeteria for a cinnamon bun. Helen enthusiastically agreed each time. And they would be gone for what seemed like much longer than a typical break period, returning each time smiling and chatting after having enjoyed each other's company. Helen was the only team member whom Erica approached to share her breaks with. Neither of them ever invited anyone else to join them, and I never saw Helen ask anyone else to share their breaks with her.

Their fast friendship put me on edge. It looked like they were creating their own private clique. It bothered me that my supervisor was now chummy with the employee who had become so argumentative and insubordinate. My instincts were telling me to be wary, but I repeatedly told myself that I was letting my imagination get out of control. And I kept waking up early, but my early-morning imaginings about The Boss were now being crowded out by my suspicions of Erica and Helen.

FEEDING

I WAS NOW responsible for data processing, something I had never done before. I relished the growth that this opportunity was giving me, but I needed help. There was a lot to do in a short time and I was barely keeping up. I was working with colleagues in other areas of the agency who had very specific skills and expertise, and I was very fortunate to be able to rely on them to walk me through what they needed. I told them that my questions were meant to ensure that their expectations were being met, but truthfully I feared being judged as incompetent. I still wanted – *needed* – to do as perfect a job as possible, and I knew well by now how people who *weren't* seen that way were judged.

Within my own team, anyone who had the necessary experience to help me was assigned to tasks that needed their expertise more urgently, including Isaac, who reported to me. I had Erica and another employee on my team, but they were as inexperienced as I was. I was only ever a step and a half ahead of them in understanding what to do before having to teach them. Plus, I still had Erica's arguing and the machinations between her and Helen swirling in the back of my head. But I saw all of this as a challenge to overcome, and overcoming it meant I had proven my worth.

I regularly told myself that I was being paranoid about Helen and Erica, that I had an overtired, overworked imagination and their cafeteria tête-à-têtes may not have had anything to do with me at all. Instead of thinking I was sane and could trust my intuition, I was sane enough to think I might be going *in*sane.

Isaac and Helen's badmouthing about Louise had worsened, comments now being made about her general competence and intelligence, and within earshot of multiple colleagues. This didn't happen frequently, but enough to show that Helen was fine with badmouthing people publicly.

This was even more evident when she spoke about The Boss. Helen did *not* like him and I never knew why. She and Isaac were tasked with trying to fix errors in the last cycle that The Boss had presided over before his promotion, for which they sometimes had to ask him about processes and decisions that might explain how the errors had occurred. In our exposed workspace, Helen and Isaac would openly mock his logic, past choices, and the pictures he had drawn to help explain how something worked. They never said The Boss's name out loud, but anyone nearby who'd been around long enough knew whom they were referring to. I felt defensive when I heard them. Despite my anger with him, I remembered the challenges he faced to get the project off the ground and keep it viable – something neither Isaac nor Helen ever witnessed – and I still respected him for that.

One day, I decided I had had enough and so I walked up to them and interrupted their badmouthing to describe some of the challenges happening at the time that led to the choices they were criticizing. I thought they wouldn't be so harsh with their comments if they understood how those decisions were necessary. That quieted them in the moment, but they were back at it a few weeks later. I explained the history to them again – and four or five times more till I lost my patience. I said to them civilly and respectfully, though I knew I sounded terse, "You two are criticizing choices made at a time when difficult decisions had to be made, which you don't know about or understand because you weren't there. And not only that, you're doing so loudly enough that people halfway down the hall can probably hear you. You need to stop." I could tell by the looks on their faces that they didn't like hearing me speak to them that way, but they stopped badmouthing him, at least when I was around.

My paranoia extended to wondering what was said about *me* in private. Helen met with me periodically over the summer to discuss my relationship with Erica, whose attacks I continued to let slide because I didn't see the point in addressing a behaviour she didn't want to change. Helen wanted to talk to me about her sometimes because of my weekly update, but usually because she wanted to tell me how upset Erica was over our most recent disagreement and that I needed to be more lenient with her.

Telling me what she "knew" about Erica's feelings confirmed my suspicions they *were* talking about me during their shared breaks. I defended myself by describing how Erica was acting towards me, how I dealt with it (or didn't), and her continued defiance. Nothing I said made a dent with Helen. According to her, Erica was really sorry about it and I should give her another chance. Again.

I eventually challenged Helen on her unqualified support of Erica. "I know you're talking about me during your shared breaks because how else would you know how Erica feels?"

"That is not true. We do not discuss you or anything work related during our breaks," Helen replied.

"Then how else would you know how Erica feels about me or our disagreements? I sit right next to you. I see you come and go together, and only for those breaks."

"Erica hasn't said anything to me. What I'm saying comes from my own observations."

Right.

I challenged Helen again at another meeting. I told her that I thought Erica was play-acting for sympathy, being rude and insubordinate to me only when Helen wasn't watching. She remained unconvinced, repeating that I give her more chances and adding that I *had* to because I was her supervisor. Helen clearly wasn't going to support me as I thought she might earlier that summer. Her unwavering support of Erica meant I had two people working against me, not one.

I had my first nightmare around this time.

I dreamt that I was standing at the foot of a grey, arched, cobblestone bridge. It crossed over a stream, and there was a grassy field on either side. I was walking from one end of the bridge to the other. When I hit the bridge's apex, I looked down over the edge into the water. I saw three pairs of feet dangling, nothing more, but knew that the feet belonged to bodies that were hanging from nooses attached to the under-belly of the bridge.

Then I woke up.

It was now August. Erica was attacking me more frequently, pointedly, and boldly as the summer continued. In one incident, she questioned my instructions during a group meeting. When I said I preferred the team to try my approach first, she retorted, "Well, it's wrong, so I'm going to do it my way instead." Helen witnessed this.

As soon as the meeting adjourned and everyone else left, I told Helen that this showed the insubordination I was getting from Erica. Helen dismissively waved her hand and said, "Oh, let Erica do what she wants," then walked out of the room. I was shocked by Helen's willingness to ignore the obvious, though I don't know why. I by now concluded that Helen only saw a victim whose behaviour could be explained away or ignored out of some misplaced need to save her from the big bad supervisor.

I continued to vent to Mark. He empathized with me, but seemed to accept all of this as something one should expect to deal with in the workplace. He had experienced his own share of toxic co-workers and supervisors, though most of it was from situations happening around him instead of directly to him. Erica's and Helen's behaviour was nothing new to him and, relative to some of what he had witnessed elsewhere, not that severe. He thought I shouldn't be as bothered by it. "You're not going to change anything," he said. "You need to accept it or leave." I couldn't do either. I wasn't going to accept behaviour that was so clearly wrong to me, nor did I feel I should leave a job that I loved because of it.

After yet another incident with Erica, I decided I was going to reclaim my role as a supervisor and meet with her to discuss her behaviour. I had obeyed Helen's entreaties long enough and with nothing positive to show for it. I approached Erica at her desk and asked if I could talk to her privately. She removed her earbuds, looked up at me indignantly, and replied, "No. And from now on I only want you to communicate with me in writing." She then put her earbuds back in her ears and turned away from me to start typing as if I wasn't there.

Wow.

I felt stunned and angry, but kept my cool and returned to my desk. There was clearly no talking to her at this point. I took a deep breath and thought about how I should react. She was the employee, which meant that her wishes had to be respected – and frankly, the silence would be an opportunity to get a break from her. A few days later, though, she emailed me asking to meet. She wrote that someone she knew had just passed away, which caused her to re-evaluate her relationships, including ours, and she wanted to see if we could reconcile.

Part of me thought that I should talk to her at that moment, but I decided not to because I didn't want to look like I was taking advantage of someone in a vulnerable state. I was also still angry and knew I needed to calm my feelings if I was to have a productive conversation with her. So I replied, in writing, that I would book a meeting for us to talk in a few days, acknowledging that both her and my emotions might be running high and a few days would give us time to work through them.

When the day arrived, I greeted her at the meeting time and suggested we walk outside, hoping that it would encourage a more relaxed conversation. She agreed, but with a cold look and curt tone. Right away I knew that something had changed since she wrote that email. On the elevator, she stood in the opposite corner from me, arms folded, lips pursed, and wouldn't look at me. I immediately felt tense and wary.

As soon as we got outside, she angrily launched into her rapid-fire judgments and criticisms but, possibly because we were outside, louder and more cutting than ever before, still stringing together multiple grievances in speedily spoken sentences. I'd take a moment after each onslaught to think about how to respond, during which she'd cut in and criticize me for not having an answer at my fingertips. I asked for specific examples, and many were either vague or something I couldn't remember, but some I knew were things that I never would have said or done and said so to her. It was then that I knew her "examples" were either made up or based on real events twisted so severely as to no longer resemble truth, creations to suit whatever argument she wanted to make. I stopped trying to remember what happened and let her words wash over me.

After two or three tours around our complex, my mental and emotional energy was sapped from the effort it took to remain constructive. Erica didn't seem to have much more to say either, so we made our way back into the building. As we did, Erica told me that she had requested to move to another desk – and added that others complained I wasn't a good listener too, though she didn't say who.

I felt like I'd been had. My patience was gone. I was done. I asked her if she wanted to go back to communicating with me only in writing, and she answered yes, to which I was grateful because I really wanted a break from her tongue-lashings at this point. I wanted – *needed* – peace and quiet to recoup from this "meeting" so that I could have the mental energy to deal with her again.

I felt nothing about her accusations and judgments because I had become so used to them that they no longer affected me – except for her comment that others had similar complaints. That stuck with me. I suspected that she had made it up just to be hurtful or to prop herself up, but it wouldn't have been responsible of me to let it slide. Dealing with Erica didn't exempt me from trying to be a good, conscientious supervisor for everyone else.

After Erica left for the day, I told Helen what she had said, on the premise that Helen wouldn't hesitate to say if others had complained about me. I didn't want to ask her, but she was the only option other than putting each of my employees on the spot by asking them individually. My stress from the meeting with Erica took over as soon as I started speaking. The calm, collected nature I had to maintain all day had no psychological energy to keep going. I started tearing up. Helen saw this and suggested that we meet the next morning to talk about it.

I had prepared myself that night by going through past conversations and body language cues with each team member in my head to detect anything that would indicate a relationship problem. Nothing struck me. I was still nervous when I arrived at work in the morning.

Helen had booked a meeting room on a different floor than where we worked. We walked in together and sat opposite each other. I began the conversation with a high-level recap of my meeting with Erica, ending with her allegation that others had complained that I was a bad listener. I asked

Helen, "Has anyone, other than Erica, ever complained about me to you?"

That's when Helen began a speech about how someone at my level and in a supervisory position was expected to meet certain competencies, and then started listing them.

Huh?

I was confused. I didn't understand where this was coming from or where it was going. I kept listening, thinking that the answer to my question was hidden somewhere in this list of competencies that she was lecturing me about. *Did someone complain that I wasn't meeting any of these? When did I fail like this? How does this answer my question?* I couldn't decipher any answers. She just kept naming behaviours, actions, and skills that she expected me to demonstrate on a regular basis, like training my employees, communicating regularly with team members and colleagues in our partner divisions, and being pleasant to be around, all in long detail with barely a pause to breathe.

But I do those things, I thought. *When didn't I?* And I knew that Helen had witnessed me do some of these things, too. My brain swirled while trying to make sense of why I was hearing all this.

When Helen took a breath, I started to ask her where this lecture was coming from but couldn't get more than a syllable out before she cut me off and continued. She was like a steamroller. I tried to interject a couple more times before she finally took an extended pause and I could get that question in. "I don't know where your comments are coming from. Why do you think that I'm not doing those things?" But instead of answering my question, she restarted the lecture as if on repeat. And I sat there, jaw dropped, again unable to cut in.

My emotional exhaustion from the day before and the nerves from that morning, not to mention having barely slept in over a year, got the better of me and I could feel myself start to cry. *Don't cry*, I told myself. I had been criticized before at work, but never on *everything* that I was or tried to be. I asked again where her opinion came from during another extended breath, but she simply repeated the lecture again. It wasn't long before my tears turned into sobs, right in front of her, as she continued steamrolling on.

When she finally finished, she asked, "How are you?" with a look of care and concern, seemingly oblivious to my tear-stained, mucous-dripping face. I asked her if she could get me some tissues from somewhere. She looked at me with surprise, cocked her head to the side and cooed a sympathetic, "Ooooh," as if to say, *Oh, poor you*, then, "I didn't realize you were crying." She left the room to find tissues for me, looking pleased to help. When she returned with them, she looked at me pitifully and asked, "Is there anything I can do to help?" I was stunned by her utter inability to recognize that her lecture was what had led to all this.

She never had answered my original question. I asked one last time if others complained about me. She looked at me with a bit of surprise and said, "No, no one other than Erica has said anything to me about you."

Then where did this lecture come from? I felt too steamrolled and emotionally exhausted to ask.

I wanted nothing more than to get out of there and away from her. Helen walked out of the room with me, chatting casually to me, as if we were on friendly terms. It was surreal. I kept quiet and let her talk, still raw from her lecture. I'm sure I still looked red and weepy, but I did my best to keep myself from becoming emotional in front of walkers-by.

The meeting lasted nearly two hours.

I spent the rest of the day trying to keep myself focused on my work, thinking it was the mature, professional thing to do. I thought leaving would make me look like I was neglecting my duties, showing I couldn't handle criticism, or whatever assumption Helen would choose to make of it. Fortunately, I was busy enough that I could distract myself, but it was still a struggle. It was also my last day before a one-week vacation. I needed to ensure that everything I was responsible for was in order before I left.

After work, I hopped on the bus to pick up my daughter from school. The morning started replaying in my head. Helen's accusations repeated and overlapped themselves like a tangled web. I knew I wasn't guilty of them, but *she* thought I was, and she evaluated my performance and had Laura's ear. The power she had to ruin me caused me a level of anxiety I hadn't known before.

I could feel my eyes well up. *Oh no, not here. Not on the bus.* I tried to repress those thoughts with something more benign, but was failing. I raced to the rear doors of the bus as soon as it approached my stop, ready to race off as soon as they opened. Once I did, I started speed walking to the school, hoping I could somehow get away from the emotional tidal wave that was coming over me.

But I couldn't. The tears started pouring. My breathing quickened and soon became laboured. Next thing I knew, I was standing still, bent over on the sidewalk, hyperventilating and crying at the same time. I tried to pull myself together because I was in public, traffic whizzing by, and halfway to my daughter's school. My mind jolted to my daughter. *She can't see you like this!* Knowing I had to shield her from my distress helped me bury my feelings, pull myself together, and continue walking to the school like a calm, happy, capable mother, not one whose four-year-old needed to worry about.

I was looking forward to my first mother-daughter trip to Mont-Tremblant. I had only one plan: to have fun with my four-year-old and focus solely on her. But what happened with Helen turned happiness and excitement into feeling dark and weighed down. The web of her lecture started unravelling, arguments being teased apart by my brain while I slept. And as that clarity developed, so did my anger – at the accusations, her blindness, and at her ability to drive me to an anxiety attack. I'd never had one before, and I was shaken by the thought that she – or anyone – could induce me into one. My pride swelled. *How dare you?* I thought. *How dare you have that kind of impact on me.*

I had to confront her claims. If I didn't, she'd continue to believe they were true and might include them in my performance evaluations. So I packed a notebook in my suitcase, determined not to let my developing clarity fade, ready to write down everything I could remember and examples to prove her wrong. During our vacation, I evacuated these thoughts onto paper while my daughter slept so they wouldn't plague me while I was with her. This gave me the mental freedom to focus on mother-daughter fun during the day.

I presented my examples to Helen when I returned. She sat stone-faced as I went through them one by one. I couldn't tell if she resented being challenged or just didn't care about what I was telling her, but I pushed through. I finished by saying, "I wish you had asked me about my work experience earlier. I hope that, next time, you'll talk to me sooner before making assumptions." Still stone-faced, she thanked me for providing her the examples and agreed that she would speak to me sooner in the future. I was fine with that response. After the impact that she had on me, I wanted as much distance from her as I could get away with.

I had two very distinct feelings: increased pride and a need to self-defend. I'd always thought of myself as a strong person, someone who could fight her own battles and keep a cool mind. That anxiety attack had hurt the image I had of myself. By challenging Helen's assumptions, I was healing my damaged pride and, in some small way, trying to come out the victor.

However, I also now felt incredibly anxious around this woman. The fact that she could drive me to an attack, judge me based on false and unchecked assumptions, and lecture me to the point of sobbing made her a professional and psychological threat. The idea of talking to her made my chest tighten. So, I erected a wall around myself for protection. I kept my conversations with her to a minimum, ignored her presence as much as I could politely get away with, and updated her about work only through email as written documentation meant she couldn't make up stories about me and my work. My guard was up with her even more so than it was with Erica, with whom I decided to continue limiting communication to "written only."

I feared going to Laura about any of this. I never forgot that The Boss had said that I had a problem with supervisors; I believed that if I raised a concern about Helen, it would be seen as me having a problem with yet another one. And since

I started reporting to Helen, I barely spoke with Laura. By this time, I could have counted on one hand the number of times I spoke with her, and usually were no more than a "good morning" as we passed each other in the corridor. She also sat on the opposite end of the team where I was, physically distant enough not to hear or see anything that was going on in our area. For months now, I had virtually no relationship with my manager, and therefore no foundation to rely on for help. I had to deal with this on my own.

Every day on the bus ride home, I'd try to shake off my emotional exhaustion by listening to whatever music I had on my phone that felt cathartic. It was usually hard rock or metal. But I had one, "Let The Sunshine In" by The Fifth Dimension, that was just *happy*. On my darker days, which were growing increasingly frequent, I'd listen to that one song on repeat for nearly the full ride home, letting the song's joyous-sounding chorus fill and lighten my soul.

Then came my second nightmare.

I was sitting in a café. In front of me was a bar, and around me were round wooden tables adorned with red and white checkered tablecloths. I was sitting at a table near the entrance. Suddenly, two men in trench coats entered, pulled out machine guns, and started spraying the room with bullets. I got down quickly, turned my table over, and hid behind it to shield myself. I prayed that I would make it out alive.

Then I woke up.

In September, Helen met with Erica and me to discuss resolving our differences. She suggested we attend Informal Conflict Management sessions, separately or together. These sessions gave a person or a group of people the opportunity to speak with a neutral facilitator to resolve interpersonal issues at work. Erica preferred joint sessions with me and I preferred to go alone, at least for now.

I knew that refusing the joint sessions wouldn't reflect well on me. I didn't care. What I wanted was distance and a tall, thick wall between myself and them, not to give them opportunities to capitalize on my psychological vulnerability. I felt that Erica would play the victim with the facilitator as I suspected she did with Helen, and would share with Helen anything I said or what the facilitator told *me* to do to mend our relationship, while being less than honest about herself. Joint sessions would have given Helen more ammunition against me.

I also didn't see myself as the problem, nor did I see Helen or Erica as people whose comments I should be taking seriously. I had never argued with someone on the street, lectured them to the point of tears, nor to my knowledge induced anyone into an anxiety attack. They didn't have the moral authority to tell me what I should change or how to behave.

A week or two later, Helen asked me to start speaking to Erica again, knowing that not speaking was Erica's idea. "She's really upset over how you haven't been talking to her. She wants to mend fences with you."

"The last time Erica told me how upset she was," I replied, "she yelled at me out on the street. And remember that me not talking to her was her idea. If she wants me to speak to her again, she should tell me so herself."

Helen dismissed what I said and tried to convince me of Erica's regret and sadness. I pushed back, Helen persisted, but in the end I wouldn't hear of it. "We all have our own way of handling things," I said.

Helen leaned back into her chair, looking surprised by the finality of my statement. "Okay," she replied.

Every day I felt like I had to be in a constant state of alert around them. Being behind and next to them meant I constantly felt their energy around me. I always felt I had to be ready to shield myself from any attack or comment that could make me feel vulnerable, while also trying to look as though nothing bothered me.

It was around this time that I started trancing, like a kind of spacing out. Trances would come at home, suddenly and involuntarily, when I had no distractions around me. They were like daytime versions of my early wake-ups, like riding on a train that I couldn't disembark from till I reached the end of the track or something grabbed my attention. They could last from a few minutes to up to an hour. I tranced almost daily.

My sleep study finally happened in October, the week before Thanksgiving, thanks to a cancellation. I came with a bag packed ready for work the next day, as I was planning to go there straight from the clinic. It didn't occur to me take the next day off or go in late. There was too much to do.

When I arrived, I stared at the clinic door from inside the car, as it suddenly dawned on me what being there meant. I knew I needed this study, and I had waited six months for it. But the waiting had kept the sleep study firmly in the back of my mind where I didn't need to think about it: arriving at the clinic made it real. And the reality was that I felt embarrassed. Ashamed. Because being there meant that I needed help, and arriving there forced me to acknowledge it. I quietly teared up in the car, realizing that I had failed at being the strong, resilient, independent person I wanted to be. After a few minutes, I got hold of my emotions, swallowed my pride, and walked into the building.

A couple of weeks later was my mid-year review with Helen. I felt on edge walking with her to the room she'd booked which, like last time, was on a different floor than where we worked. I didn't know what to expect. Nothing had been said about my work since I'd confronted her about my competencies and, though I expected Helen to raise my issues with Erica, she hadn't mentioned Erica to me in weeks.

Helen appeared tense. We sat down directly across from each other. She held up a piece of paper and said, "I have your review written on this paper. I will be reading off of it to make sure I don't forget to say anything." Then she started reciting my accomplishments, sounding cold and forced in tone, almost robotic in cadence, barely looking up from the paper. I didn't mind it; I just wanted to get through this. I responded by simply nodding and thanking her for the recognition.

Still tense and robotic, she then said, "I have been made aware that you have trouble sleeping. I want to acknowledge that this could be behind your behavioural issues. Do you need an accommodation?" She stared back at me, coldly.

My behavioural issues? I was flabbergasted to hear this from someone who had driven me to sobs two months prior. And Erica was the only person on the team whom I'd ever told about my sleep issues, so this reconfirmed that Helen and Erica gossiped about me. But Helen's mention of accommodation made me fearful. Employees who are given accommodation are those who need help meeting their work expectations. It could be something like reduced hours, a reduced workload, longer deadlines, or anything of that nature for someone dealing with a physical or mental health issue. Helen's current tone and the impact she had on me in August made her the last person I was going to confess any vulnerability to.

I deflected by telling her that I suspected she got that information from Erica.

"No, I figured this out myself because you occasionally look tired in meetings," she replied.

True or not, that was a flimsy rationale for assuming I had a significant sleep issue and so I used that to deflect more. "We all get tired, Helen, even you sometimes. What should matter is if it's causing a problem in my work. Has it?"

"No, your work is fine," she begrudgingly admitted.

"Then as long as my work is fine, how much sleep I'm getting shouldn't be a concern," I said, calmly and coolly. "If anything changes and I need an accommodation, I will let you know." Helen glared at me, lips pursed. She looked as though she expected me to confide in her and was angry that I didn't.

That's when the meeting went off the rails. Helen brought up Erica. Nothing she said surprised me – it was the same pro-Erica view I'd heard all summer – and she capped it by raising the fact that I had not been speaking to Erica. She said it could be interpreted as harassment. "I told Labour Relations and they told me I should give you an action plan."

I felt blindsided.

An action plan is a disciplinary measure for bad behaviour. It outlines what the employee did to deserve being disciplined and what they must do to demonstrate that they won't repeat it. It was a tool that, as far as I saw, was used to punish the workplace's worst performers and biggest abusers. It also becomes part of an employee's permanent record.

Not speaking with Erica could be considered harassment? Helen never hinted that she thought calling Labour Relations would be necessary. I was scared. I had heard of Labour Relations but had never had to use them. I was never quite sure what they did – until now, and in the worst way possible.

I had to fight back. I reminded Helen that one of the rules about performance reviews is that nothing said should come as a surprise to the employee. "Consulting Labour Relations and threatening an action plan after a month of silence definitely qualifies as a surprise," I said. "You should have said something to me sooner for you to put this in my review."

"I have to show management that I'm taking action to resolve the situation."

She meant The Director and The Boss. My heart skipped a beat. I asked her what they knew. Helen's answer hit me hard: "They know *everything*," she said with satisfaction.

Now I was *really* scared. I still admired The Boss despite how I had tried to separate myself from him. My brain started doing somersaults wondering what else she might have told him and if he believed her.

I felt everything stacking up against me now. *Am I fighting against senior management now, too? Is my career in jeopardy?* I defended myself by reminding Helen it was Erica who had asked me not to speak to her.

"It doesn't matter," Helen replied, "You have to keep speaking with her even if she asks you not to."

Huh?

"Don't I have a right to protect myself?"

"No, you don't," Helen answered, her voice now quite

raised. "As the supervisor, it is your responsibility to fix the relationship no matter how badly that employee is treating you."

No piece of me believed that a supervisor should accept verbal abuse, nor that anyone should be expected to fix a relationship with someone who didn't want it fixed. "It takes two to tango. If Erica doesn't want to work on the relationship with me, there isn't much I can do."

Helen's agitation grew. "It doesn't matter," she snapped back, her voice getting louder and her face looking increasingly angry and impatient. The snappiness in her replies made me wonder if she truly was right in everything she said. I kept reminding myself to look and sound calm.

"If you want to avoid an action plan, then you must meet with me weekly to tell me how you are repairing your relationship with Erica."

"I don't know how to fix the relationship," I answered. "I've done everything I can think of, even giving her all the chances you told me to. I tried and failed."

Helen stood up, slammed her hands on the table, and yelled, "*Try harder!*"

I paused, startled by her sudden outburst. I knew I had to remain calm. "I don't know what else *to* try. Do *you* know?"

"*Figure it out!*" she yelled again, dismissively waving her arm in the air at me. I laughed inwardly at the irony of her being angry at me for not knowing what to do when she didn't either. Oddly, seeing her lose control of herself felt calming. It was as if her behaviour suddenly validated every intuition I had that she couldn't be trusted and that I was right to keep my guard up with her. There was a brief pause, during which Helen looked as though she knew she should not have stood and yelled. She sat back down, acting as if nothing had happened.

Helen moved on to The Boss. She said that I had no right to lecture her and Isaac publicly about badmouthing him. "It was a private conversation that didn't involve you," she continued, "and shows that you don't know how to be diplomatic." This from the person who just yelled at me over the table?

I felt as firmly in the right about this now as I did then. "I *was* diplomatic with you and Isaac multiple times when I'd approach you both and explain what had been happening at that time in the survey. I hoped that it would tell you that you were criticizing something you weren't around for and didn't know. I lost my patience because *you weren't getting the hint.* And though you never mentioned him by name, anyone overhearing you who's been around long enough would know who you were talking about, and I think you'll agree with me that it's not a good idea to publicly badmouth someone in senior management who has power over your career."

Helen stood up again, slammed her hands on the table and yelled, "*If I want to vent, I get to!*"

The fact that I was successfully keeping my cool while she wasn't meant that I was more mature and professional than her. It amazed me how she was the supervisor and I wasn't.

Yet she *was* my supervisor. She had the power to write whatever she wanted in my review, tell management whatever she wanted about me, and expect to be believed. Helen calmed herself and sat back down, but she was still angry. The meeting continued with more false assumptions about my inadequacies that I had examples to prove wrong. She ended the meeting by telling me she was going to dock me on two of the four behavioural competencies in my review and include a recommendation that I seek psychological help.

I did my best during the rest of the day to distract myself with work. I didn't want to leave early. Doing so would show that she had gotten to me, and I wasn't about to let her have that satisfaction. But on the way home, just as in August, my brain swirled around everything she'd said. I was scared about how much of "everything" The Boss and The Director knew. The idea that The Boss could believe anything Helen said about me put me into a state of panic. I tried and failed to bury those thoughts while on the bus ride home and, in nearly the same place, time, and manner as the first, I had my second anxiety attack.

I met with Helen the next day to give her examples of when I showed the abilities she accused me of not having and the names of people who could back me up. I also told her that writing that I should seek psychological help in my review was inappropriate because using those services was confidential and senior management could access employees' reviews. Helen agreed to remove those points from my review. But the threat of the action plan still loomed, and I still had to meet with her weekly about Erica.

I asked her to clarify what exactly The Boss and The Director knew.

"Oh, I don't know what they know," she replied.

"You told me yesterday that they know 'everything.' That implies you had a conversation with them."

"I only spoke to Laura. I'm assuming that she spoke with them."

I felt my jaw drop.

Later, I conducted Erica's mid-year review. Helen told me that if I wanted to evade an action plan, then I had to show I was working on my relationship with her, starting with being kind to her during her review. As usual, Erica was cutting, cold, and argumentative, but the threat of the action plan motivated me to try to have some kind of conversation with her. A full half hour passed before Erica began to soften and speak respectfully to me. I still docked Erica on one competency (I don't remember which one), which was all I thought I could get away with.

When we were done, I went to Helen's desk to tell her how Erica behaved during that first half hour. I wanted to remind her how unreasonable her expectation to fix this relationship was. Helen said nothing. She simply turned away from me, looked back at her screen, and pretended I wasn't there.

The second anxiety attack made me realize that I needed help. I was terrified of the possibility that I could have a third, and maybe closer to the school or, worse yet, in front of my daughter or her teachers. I had to get a handle on this. In November 2016, through my workplace's Employee Assistance Program (EAP), I started seeing a therapist. And on December 22, 2016, the results of my sleep study came in: insomnia with sleep stage misperception.

SURVIVING

SLEEP STAGE MISPERCEPTION is pretty much what it sounds like – you think you're in a stage of sleep that you're not actually in. For me, staying asleep was the problem and, though I always thought I was awake at 3:30 in the morning, I wasn't. During my sleep study, someone walked into my room at 1 a.m. to adjust some of the connections on my head, letting a bright light shine into the room. I remembered being awake from that point on. However, when I shared that with the doctor, he told me that I actually went back to sleep almost immediately, but remained in a very light stage of sleep. Light enough that my brain would be doing somersaults, but still technically asleep. This probably explains how I could never will myself to stop my imaginings and get out of bed, and why I always seemed to get just barely enough sleep to function (albeit very poor-quality sleep). He referred me to a psychologist who specialized in sleep disorders.

All this time I thought I was indulging in early-morning

fantasies that I was too weak to pull myself out of. I wasn't. I was trapped.

I spent November and December focused on pushing through my tasks and saying whatever I needed to get out from under the threat of an action plan. I did this with the help of my therapist from the EAP. EAP was a free service offered to employees that they, or their immediate family members, could access for short-term psychological support.

I liked that my therapist was a pragmatic person. She and I focused on my unresolved feelings with The Boss and Number 2, my anxiety around Helen, and trying to detach me emotionally from everything that happened. She tried to guide me towards letting go of the questions I could never answer about The Boss and how to behave around Helen so that I could work through her action plan threat while protecting myself emotionally.

In the meantime, I met with Helen every week. I reported what I was doing and she judged if she was satisfied with it. I started talking to Erica again and offered to do joint Informal Conflict Management sessions with her to work out our differences, but she refused. Helen didn't seem bothered by Erica's refusal and was simply content that I offered. Erica's move request was also granted and she began sitting with Sam. It became a lot easier for me to deal with her because I no longer had to see her glares or hear her criticisms. She was going to transfer to Sam's team around the new year, which meant I only had to be pleasant and bide my time.

I didn't address any issues with her because I wanted to avoid all possibility of conflict. After roughly two months of me telling Helen how I was nice to Erica, coinciding with

Erica just having transferred to Sam's group, Helen told me that she was no longer threatening me with an action plan. She was satisfied that I had made an effort to improve our relationship which, because it was under her weekly "tutelage" of me, also demonstrated that I trusted her judgment.

Sure.

As soon as that threat was gone, I went back to putting as much distance between myself and them as I could get away with. I could hear Erica badmouthing me to Sam almost as soon as she moved to his area, though only the first couple of sentences before her voice became a whisper. I told Helen about this, who answered that she couldn't do anything because she never witnessed it herself.

I felt alone. There wasn't anyone in a position of authority I could talk to about what had been happening. I didn't know if Laura believed Helen's allegations against me. The Boss might assume that this was simply me having a problem with yet another supervisor, and I was worried that he heard and believed Helen's accusations. No one in management – Laura, The Boss, or The Director – had ever approached me to discuss what was happening and I didn't know if that was because they actually knew nothing, didn't believe Helen's accusations, or – what I was most afraid of – believed them and wrote me off. I was too scared to find out.

I coped by reaching out to people outside my team. I would say hello and chat for a few minutes with some colleagues while on my way to the kitchen to make my morning tea, or make small talk with them at lunch when it wasn't nice enough to walk outside. I was also involved in my division's social committee, which helped me develop relationships with colleagues outside my team. I needed to keep reminding myself that all the toxicity was just in my little corner of the floor. I basked in the camaraderie of every small chat I had with someone, even if it was only for a minute or two.

So, if everything was so bad, why hadn't I left by then? How was this job worth anxiety attacks and insomnia? Work required enough time and focus to keep me from trancing. Trances came at home when I had nothing distracting me. I feared that leaving work entirely would mean more undistracted time and, therefore, nothing to keep me from living in this mental state, not to mention make me look like I wasn't tough enough to handle pressure or difficult people. And I remembered the stress and instability in my work that Louise's absences caused. We were already short staffed. If my or another part of the project suffered because someone had to cover for me, then that suffering would have been my fault.

But it was getting harder keeping the tension to myself. During the Christmas holidays, with Helen gone on vacation, I decided to ask Laura for advice. Despite my anxiety, I felt I had reached a point where I had more to gain than lose by speaking with her.

I didn't get into the yelling or the anxiety attacks, because I feared that would make me look like I was complaining or attacking instead of trying to get constructive advice. Instead, I explained that Helen often made false assumptions about me and I didn't know where they came from. I wanted to keep my personal life private in order to prevent more of this. Laura answered, "If you want to demonstrate the competencies expected of you, then you need to have a personal relationship with her."

What?

"Um, I think I wasn't clear," I answered. "I don't mean

never speaking to her or being pleasant. I mean not talking about my weekend, home life, or anything that doesn't have to do with work. Be pleasant and respectful, but keep conversations to work only."

"You can't do that," she continued. "You have to have a personal relationship with her."

I was dumbfounded. I never expected anyone in a management position to tell me that I was expected to have a personal relationship with my supervisor, let alone with anyone else I worked with. I felt let down and unsupported. I ended the conversation by asking her for advice on how to develop that relationship. She told me to contact Informal Conflict Management for guidance, because she had none.

2017

I began seeing the psychologist whom the sleep clinic referred me to. I asked my therapist from Employee Assistance to transfer my records over so the psychologist could get caught up on what was happening at work. We discussed my sleep patterns and how I felt unable to get up.

She instructed me to begin a sleep diary and to follow these points for getting my sleep back on track:

1. The bed is meant for only two things: sleep and sex

2. Doing anything else in bed associates being in bed with wakefulness (so, no reading, no looking at a cellphone, etc.)

3. I shouldn't go to bed until I felt the pressure to sleep

The last point came with a rule: don't go to bed until midnight. If I felt sleepy before then, I had to keep myself awake. She explained to me that the way to get my sleep back on track was to create more sleep deprivation. Right now, my body didn't feel any urgency to get more sleep because I was getting enough to function. However, by keeping myself awake and becoming more sleep deprived, my body would crave more sleep and therefore start to sleep longer. We were starting with a midnight bedtime but, over time, we would move that to 11:30, then 11, and so on until I could reliably sleep for eight hours straight. As we worked on this, we talked about The Boss, Helen, and everything else going on that was causing me to ruminate so early.

I also started meeting with a facilitator from Informal Conflict Management. I told Laura about it because I wanted her to know that I took her advice seriously and because I didn't need more enemies. She was pleased because it showed I was willing to work on my relationship with Helen.

But was Helen going to work on it with me?

The facilitator and I focused on combatting my anxiety around Helen. One of the first assignments was to say hello to her in the morning. It sounded simple, but every fibre in my being wanted to avoid this woman. Saying hello to her would be removing a few bricks from the wall that I had built to protect myself. I feared becoming vulnerable.

Nevertheless, I promised I would try, and one morning I did it. In spite of my tightening chest and jaw, racing heart, and my brain telling me she didn't deserve such kindness, I said good morning – and she said the same in return. And that was it. Inconsequential. We both returned to our desks, but it still took me a few minutes to calm myself down and relax. *There, done*, I thought. *I can report back that I completed my assignment. We can move on.*

My facilitator "rewarded" me by increasing the difficulty: make small talk. I loathed this challenge more than the first. On Monday I asked how her weekend had been. She was polite, but curt, and I was more than fine with that. I told my facilitator that I didn't see a point in these exercises because it didn't seem like Helen wanted to be friendly. My facilitator said that this wasn't about being friends: the goal was to reduce my anxiety around Helen enough so that if I ever truly needed her for something important, I would have the emotional strength to approach her. I *was* starting to feel less anxious around Helen and didn't feel the need to avoid her as much as I had before. But I still didn't like or trust her.

In late January, Laura announced that she would be leaving the agency. The Boss would move to our section of the floor and be interim manager till her replacement was found. I wasn't sure how to react. I wondered if it would be an opportunity for some ice to thaw between The Boss and me. Despite all of the rejection, I felt a sense of comfort knowing he would be nearby as I hoped his presence would improve discipline on the team and discourage the badmouthing. We had a team get-together to wish Laura well when she left. I baked a cake for it, something I typically did to celebrate birthdays on the team. Helen looked perturbed when she saw me bring it in, and didn't come to the get-together.

Meanwhile, I was keeping myself awake till 11:30 at night (I never made it to midnight). I slept until 5 or 5:30 a.m., which was just a bit earlier than when I needed to wake up for work. As a result, I wasn't running through my imagination as much in bed, nor coming into work reeling from emotions that had been building since 3:30 a.m. My head and emotions didn't suddenly clear nor did I start perceiving past or current events in a new light, but nothing was being *added* to it now. I wasn't coming into work on high alert. My brain was starting to calm down.

This helped me practice the advice my facilitator was giving me. I was still saying hello to Helen and engaging in brief, very impersonal small talk when I could muster the mood and nerve to do so. My calmer brain helped because I wasn't lugging around 3:30 a.m. baggage with me when I approached her. I simply took those moments as they came.

Then one day, as my facilitator had anticipated, I needed to speak to Helen about something. My colleague Mylène was going to leave the team. Helen suggested that we buy her a card and gift. I was coincidentally at the mall that night for other reasons, so I took advantage of it by looking for a card. I saw one I thought Mylène would like.

Then anxiety set in. I stood there, staring at the card for what felt like an eternity, debating whether or not I should buy it. I feared that Helen would get upset if I didn't consult her first. *This is pathetic*, I thought. *Have you become so afraid of Helen that you won't even buy a card?* Then I reminded myself how rarely I made it to the mall, that I should take advantage of being there, and how unlikely it would be that Helen would also buy a card that night. I bought it. I started passing it around early the next morning so I could get some signatures before Mylène arrived.

I told Helen about the card once she came in: she had already bought one herself. I was surprised, and she looked annoyed. I explained honestly that I wouldn't have stepped in if I'd known her plan. It made no difference in her mood. She was cold to me for the rest of the day, and I was nervous around her once again.

After some reflection, I decided that the next day was an opportunity to apply my facilitator's advice about learning to confront Helen. I approached her at her desk and said that I got the impression that she wasn't happy about me buying the card. I asked her if we could go somewhere to talk about it. She turned her chair to face me, leaned back in it, looked at me full in the eyes stone-faced, and said, "I don't know what you're talking about." Everything about her was cold as ice.

As a gesture of good will I let Helen pick out the gift, but unfortunately I found out that the store from which Helen suggested buying a gift card would be closing in a few months. When I told Helen and offered a different gift suggestion, she again looked annoyed, stormed away down the corridor, and yelled back, "*Handle it yourself!*" I was initially stunned by her carelessness in yelling at someone in front of dozens of people at work, but ultimately I just felt resigned to the injustice that allowed someone who behaved like this to manage people. I thought, *I can't believe I'm putting effort into you.*

I would not have approached Helen and tried to find a solution if I was still ruminating at 3:30 a.m. I would have been too nervous to approach her or too defensive to want to propose a compromise. However, my facilitator's guidance helped me figure out how to approach Helen and my improved sleep gave me the psychological coolness to do it.

Helen went on vacation shortly after this. For each day she was gone, I walked in feeling lighter and more relaxed than I had in a long time. I didn't have to worry about her blowing up or practicing small talk with her. I could just do my job and *be*. I think I even laughed a bit more. I appreciated every moment of those days.

The beginning of the end came, by way of Sam.

He and I were selected to promote the project to junior university researchers. It involved a bit of travel and the opportunity to present with someone I liked. I was excited and imagined that Sam and I would have fun together on this mini trip. Laura shared this happy news with us before she left, but also mentioned that The Boss had originally selected only one of us to go. She said that she thought that both of us were equally deserving and should be offered the opportunity, and so argued to send us both. Laura never said whom it was The Boss preferred.

Sam and I created the presentation together. When it came time to decide who would speak for which slide, I suggested a split that I thought would give us each an equal share of time, but discovered I was wrong when we ran it through and learned his part lasted only a fraction of mine. As soon as we finished, I acknowledged how uneven our times were and offered to redivide the presentation. But he was already mad.

I suggested other ways to divide the presentation, which he rejected, saying petulantly and stubbornly, "No, you do all the talking; I'll just change the slides."

I ignored his tone. "I don't think that's fair to you, Sam. You should have an equal part. We can work this out. Is there a way you'd like to split the slides?"

"No," he answered, still with attitude. "You do the talking; I'll change the slides."

The presentation was now in jeopardy. It would look bad if we appeared at odds with each other and so we needed to work this out, but I knew Sam was proud and wouldn't change his mind easily. I needed help. Laura was no longer with us and Helen was on vacation. The only person left whom I could go to was The Boss, whom I hadn't spoken to in months. I didn't believe he would help me, but I knew he liked and supported Sam so, to encourage him to step in, I framed the request by asking him to help Sam and ensure that the project looked good to the public. He agreed to intervene and offered to set up a meeting with all of us for the next day. I thought it would be better if The Boss spoke with Sam privately. "If Sam feels put on the spot or gets the slightest hint that I went to you, he'll go on the offensive."

"I don't think he'd do that," The Boss replied. "I can ask about the split in a way that sounds casual and he won't know that you came to me. Everything will be fine." I still felt uneasy. Would he really go on the attack in front of The Boss?

The Boss, Sam and I met the next day. When The Boss put his plan into action, Sam quickly answered, "She'll do all the talking and I'll change the slides." I was stunned by how openly he said that: it didn't make him look good.

"Unless you have another suggestion as to how this should be presented," I added.

"I would like both of you to present," The Boss said. "I'd like you two to work out a split that will have both of you present equally." I agreed and asked Sam if we could work out a fair split.

That's when Sam lit up. He refused right in front of The Boss to work with me and then turned to face me, eyes full of anger, and announced, "There are some things that he should know about you." He immediately began a tirade of anger and character assassination. I had no idea where this was all coming from. He occasionally looked at The Boss when he spoke, but directed most of his gaze at me, staring me down while speaking with a condescending viciousness in his voice. The Boss remained silent.

I struggled to remain composed but, after several minutes of non-stop attacks, I had to leave and hide in a neighbouring room to calm myself. Sam's non-stop brazenness, the viciousness in his voice, and my sleep deprivation led me to feeling panic and distress. I had been in treatment for six weeks at this point, with some improvement, but far from "cured."

I remembered a deep breathing technique that my facilitator had taught me. I held one hand against my chest, another against my stomach, and slowly breathed in and out, feeling my stomach and chest move up and down as I did so. I tried to calm my fast and laboured breathing, but was anxious about being away from the meeting so long that The Boss would think I wasn't coming back. So I calmed myself down *somewhat* and rejoined the meeting. I hoped that, during my absence, the tension would have de-escalated and The Boss would have told Sam to lower his viciousness a notch. But when I sat down The Boss said, "I want you to know that we didn't talk about you or the presentation while you were away." That might have been to assure me that I wasn't being discussed behind my back, but it also meant that Sam's behaviour hadn't been addressed.

This apparently emboldened Sam, because without skipping a beat he picked up right where he'd left off and continued to attack me. He accused me of fighting with people on the team, mistreating Erica, and being the reason why Isaac wanted to leave the team. And he kept hammering at me till

I started crying. The Boss continued to remain silent, staring into his notebook.

Sam smiled smugly at The Boss when he finished, seemingly proud of his skewering. I took this moment to regain what composure I could and defend myself. "I am not fighting with everyone on the team. Have you witnessed any fights?"

"No," Sam begrudgingly answered.

"As for Erica," I continued, "Remember that there are two sides to every story. I assure you there is a lot that you don't know about, but which I won't go into because it's a private matter between her and me. As for Isaac, this is the first I've heard about him wanting to leave, so I can't comment. I can't believe you would think this of me because of one mistake. We were friends. I thought you knew me better than that." I added that I hoped this would be a fun trip for us and apologized for any misunderstanding, insisting that it was never my intention to upset him. Then I broke down again. Sam looked stone cold at me, then at The Boss. The Boss stated that each of us could have done better to work together, then walked out of the room with Sam, leaving me crying by myself.

I decided to eat my lunch in the kitchen that day. When I walked in, there was The Boss. I didn't want to see him but I feared looking silly or melodramatic if I left, so I sat at the table next to him while I ate my lunch. I knew I looked miserable. I hoped he would say something to me about that morning, but he didn't even acknowledge that I was there.

My brain did loops trying to figure out how this had happened, how Sam developed such animosity towards me. His reference to Erica confirmed that she'd been badmouthing me to him, but I felt it would have taken more than that to turn him against me. Was this unresolved stress from the last year or possibly new stress now? Did he wonder if it was me whom The Boss wanted to send and not him? Maybe, because of the success of his paper last year, he thought he should be doing the presentation himself and resented having to share.

When Helen returned from vacation the following Monday, she met with me to say that The Boss had told her what happened and tasked her to deal with it. "I'm going to speak with Sam about how he behaved. It wasn't acceptable for him to bring other people into his argument. He should have expressed his own opinions only."

But driving me to tears in front of The Boss was okay? I was tempted to challenge her, but knew I needed her on my side.

"In the meantime, I want you to be more understanding towards him. It's completely understandable he'd react as he did because you asked for help."

So Sam's behaviour is my fault?

Still not wanting to pick a fight, I asked Helen to propose using Informal Conflict Management to sort out our differences. I wasn't concerned about being painted the bad guy as I had been with Erica, and I thought a show of concern would warm Helen to my side. I also remembered how stressed Sam was in 2015 and genuinely wondered if he was going through something similar again. I made these suggestions not so much out of empathy for him but, if something really was wrong, to prevent him from lashing out again. We also still had a presentation to get through. Helen said that she would ask him about his stress and raise my suggestion of Informal Conflict Management.

In the meantime, I wasn't speaking to Sam. His attacks had cut me too deeply to feel safe around him. Regardless of why he treated me the way he did, the smug look on his face then, and the lack of remorse since, told me that he felt justified in his actions. Mark was disappointed in Sam's behaviour. He remembered the concern we had for Sam and the lunchtime walks we took him on. "It's a shame," he said, "that he doesn't pay it forward. Now we know what his true colours are."

I had a follow-up meeting with Helen to hear about her talk with Sam. Unsurprisingly, he refused to do Informal Conflict Management with me. She said that he also told her he was not under any stress, did not require assistance, and that he had a great deal of respect for me. I told Helen that attacking someone's character and driving them to tears in front of The Boss did not demonstrate respect, and that rejecting my offer meant it was now up to him to mend the relationship: I shouldn't be the only one making an effort and I couldn't keep putting myself at psychological risk.

"I need to protect myself psychologically from any more attacks by him," I said. Helen said nothing about that, and when I asked what she would do if she were in my position, she said she didn't know.

I saw this situation as an opening to get help for the team. The badmouthing and character attacks proved that the concerns I'd raised the previous year were true. "This shows that we don't know how to deal with conflict constructively," I told her. "I think we need to revisit the code of conduct and look into getting someone from Informal Conflict Management to help the team."

Helen refused again, saying, "I'm afraid that, if we do that, unkind things will be said and cliques will be formed." *The cliques are already here*, I thought. "What happened with Sam is an isolated incident," she continued. "I don't see the need to bring in someone for the team when this is just between you two." But the fact that Sam brought up alleged statements from Erica and an allegation about Isaac showed it wasn't just between us. Helen just didn't want to admit it.

More than a month passed between that meeting with The Boss and the last meeting with Helen. That's how long it festered without any resolution. The presentation went well. Sam and I were good together when we had to be in public, but I avoided him as much as I could otherwise and he did not reach out to me.

My mental state hit a new low. Erica was on the back-burner and I was learning how to handle Helen, but I didn't have the emotional strength to cope with Sam. I resented Helen's regular tête-à-têtes with Erica or Isaac instead of working, and Erica's spending large chunks of her day social-izing without consequence. I was tired of putting everything I could into a project while being attacked by people who weren't pulling their weight, being made responsible for fixing relationships with people who only attacked in return, and resentful at Laura and Helen for telling me to be more sympa-thetic or do more of … *whatever* when they themselves didn't know what to do.

And yet despite all this, a large part of me still wanted to stay. I was roughly halfway through the processing phase, with maybe eighteen months till the end. I wanted to develop the knowledge and skills that this experience would give me. It was still my dream project, I still loved what I did, and after having been on this team for nearly seven years, I felt connected here. There were people on the floor whom I had known for years and didn't want to leave.

I needed more than an ally. I needed a guide.

ESCAPING

I DECIDED TO find a mentor. This was typically someone in the management or executive ranks who was paired with a junior employee to provide career advice. I wanted someone who could advise me about how to deal with the interpersonal issues within the team. As good as my psychologist and facilitator were, they weren't living my reality, nor did they have any inside knowledge that could help me understand where I stood within my workplace. Did senior management know about everything that was happening? Did I have any allies here who could help me get through this? I wanted someone who was neutral, nearby, knew me, and would give me objective advice with my best interests at heart.

I wanted The Boss, or at least the version of him who I had before the Number 2 came along. But he was gone. So, I asked The Director for help. I was nervous because I feared that she'd heard and believed Helen's accusations about me, but she sat in the social committee meetings with me and saw,

I hoped, how well I interacted with everyone there. If not, then I was so close to rock bottom that I felt I had nothing to lose anyway. I was relieved when she offered to find a mentor for me and, for the first time in years, I felt supported. But I knew that I needed someone nearby. I told her about my situation so she could understand what I was looking for and why, but instead broke down crying and said I was considering leaving.

I recounted the last two years of my life with the team, from the difficulties with Erica up to Sam's attacks, including my insomnia diagnosis and two anxiety attacks. I told her that I hadn't come to her, or anyone, earlier because Helen had told me that she and The Boss knew of her accusations against me and I feared Helen was believed. The Director told me that none of what I shared, nor Helen's accusations, had reached her before now.

She looked concerned throughout and was very patient with me. She told me that I needed to take care of myself and would talk to Helen about what was going on within the team. She said firmly that I did not deserve to be yelled at and that she took my allegations very seriously. There was kindness in her voice, and she said all the supportive things I hoped someone would say. I was convinced that she cared and would do something to address what was going on. My only concern was about her speaking to Helen about my allegations. I told The Director that Helen often considered interpretations to be facts. It felt like a weight was taken off my shoulders knowing that someone else, and in a position of power, was now involved.

I told her that, if I were to have a mentor after all, it would need to be someone on the floor. I threw out The Boss's name as someone who might be good because of my previous working relationship with him.

At the start of May, I began a very fun and active two-week vacation. I didn't have time to think about work or to trance, and was too tired by the end of the day to ruminate at 3:30 in the morning.

Halfway through this busy, distracting trip, I decided to leave the team. I was sitting on the bed, waiting to go out to dinner, surrounded by the quiet of the room and the sounds of my husband getting ready in the washroom. Out of the blue, a question popped into my head: *Who am I doing this for?*

I felt a detachment and a clarity for the first time that I could remember. This was undoubtedly due to being away from work and sleeping through the night. I felt compelled to use this state of mind to answer the question. I realized I was staying for myself, for the experience I could still gain and my attachment to the project. But was I gaining enough to make it worth the insomnia, the anxiety attacks, and all the other emotional upheaval that I experienced? No. Did I see any potential for improvement? Maybe. My relationship with Helen was improving and I could continue to work on it, but her continued bias toward Erica and Sam meant I'd remain in a toxic work environment that wasn't going to go away anytime soon, and I felt so damaged by her at this point that I didn't have the will to work things out.

And just like that, I knew I needed to leave.

I returned to work in mid-May. During my vacation, the team had acquired a new manager, Nancy. She had just been promoted to the position.

Nancy told me that Sam had found errors in my work. I never learned if he was told to go through my work or if he acted on his own. Nancy wanted weekly meetings with him, Helen, and me to discuss what we were working on, beginning with what Sam had dug up while I was away, whatever that was.

I wasn't surprised that Sam would want to discredit me, nor that Helen would go along with it. But the dirtiness around it angered me. I felt like they went digging for worms while I was away and they left a hole big enough for my body to fit in, with a tombstone erected at the head with my name on it.

Before the first meeting, I told Nancy what had happened with Sam in March and never been resolved. "I don't want to be at these meetings," I explained. "I believe he will use them as opportunities to attack me again. And I don't trust Helen to be an impartial party in this, considering my history with her."

"It sounds like more should have been done to resolve this situation," Nancy began, "but it's important that you are present since this is your file. I want you to be there."

When we met, Helen came armed with spreadsheets she had created, filled with multiple tables with multiple rows and multiple columns, and asked me to explain why certain numbers didn't reconcile. Still not ever having learned what was wrong nor having seen these spreadsheets before, I didn't immediately understand what I was looking at. I stared at the sheets for what felt like forever before asking Helen to explain what she put together. Even then, I still didn't know how to answer her. I felt blindsided and stupid, and that might have been the point. After the meeting I returned to my desk but they remained behind. I couldn't help but think that they were talking about me.

On May 24, 2017, I went to The Director, paperwork ready, asking permission to seek an assignment elsewhere in the agency. She approved. All I needed now was to find another position to go to.

I eventually realized that I had made a mistake in one of my processes, which made one of my calculations different from Sam's in the last cycle. Both cycles had to use the same methodology. However, Sam's method didn't make sense to me either. I argued that my process, albeit inconsistent with his, provided a more accurate picture of the project's results.

During all of this, I did my best to avoid speaking to Sam. I felt he would use anything he could against me and I didn't want to give him that opportunity. Every time he spoke in one of those meetings, his tone bordered on aggression. He never looked at me unless he was accusing me of something, which he did with an angry stare, after which he would show the same smug smile to Nancy and Helen that he had shown to The Boss, as if to say, *I just proved how wrong she is!* I was sure that he was trying to ruin me professionally by turning management against me.

Sam wasn't going to let this issue rest until he got his way. No matter whose method was best, both cycles needed to be consistent, even if consistently wrong, because our clients can't have faith in our product if they don't trust or understand how we produced it. So I suggested to Nancy, privately, that we use Sam's method so we could move on. "He's like a dog with a bone in his mouth that he won't give up till he gets his way. I'm willing to redo the work using his method so we can make this go away."

Nancy refused. "I want to respect the work you did," she said.

"I appreciate hearing that but I think that will make this last longer than it should. How about this: Helen is a neutral party. Have her go through each of our methods and determine which one should be used." Nancy agreed. I didn't think Helen was neutral nor did I trust her to take my side, but putting the issue in her hands meant I could forget about it for a little while.

Throughout this time, thanks to my improved sleep, I was gradually re-evaluating my first impressions of Helen. The listening and empathy she showed that I first thought were her trying to be a supportive friend I now started to believe were an attraction to drama and/or a desire to be someone's saviour. To me, she adopted the role of Erica's saviour and defender soon after we discussed her intervention in the disagreement between Erica and me. I assumed that Helen offered her help, just like she did me, and Erica accepted it, beginning a string of play-acting to get Helen's sympathy, handing Helen the saviour role she wanted.

Helen's attraction to drama was also evident in her inexplicable ability to make up stories about me. Where could those stories come from except her own imagination, stories to fuel her need to be that saviour? She also seemed to enjoy the drama of surprising me with spreadsheets in front of Nancy and Sam. The sooner I could get away from her, the better.

Just before this, The Boss had moved to sit in our section. Seeing him there every day reminded me of my meeting with him and Sam and the unanswered questions from two years ago, compounding the unresolved situations and raw emotions I dealt with from Erica, Helen, and Sam. Together, they were too much for me to deal with. I needed to resolve at least one of them to feel some peace, and I thought that enough time had passed with The Boss that maybe this was the one to resolve.

But my psychologist advised against reaching out to him. She was concerned that my emotions were going to be too much for me to handle and that I'd say over-revealing things that could damage me professionally. She was right, but I also knew that my brain would keep tormenting me until I confronted the cause. I weighed the potential consequences that my psychologist warned me about against more mental torment and decided to initiate the conversation that I'd wanted nearly two years ago. Being approved to leave, though I still hadn't found an assignment, meant I wouldn't have to live with the consequences forever should things go badly.

He agreed to meet to discuss issues with the team and I booked us for the next day. I was nervous, fearing that I might lose control of my emotions and look like a fool. That evening, I worked on organizing what I wanted to say and how best to say it, believing it would help me stay focused and rational during our meeting.

But during the meeting, the pent-up emotions were too much for logic to overcome. I became a blubbering mess as I described everything that happened in 2015.

"Why did you wait till now to tell me about any of this?"

"I tried, multiple times," I replied, listing them.

"I don't remember any of those and I had no idea you were thinking any of this." He paused. "I try to maintain a healthy detachment from people at work." He might have been hinting that I should do the same. The Boss offered to meet again in a few weeks about how to move on. We would focus on everything that had happened with Sam, Helen, and Erica. I came out of the meeting disappointed that I couldn't keep my emotions under control and feared that I got more personal than I should have, but also feeling the calmest I had been in a long, long time.

We met again at the end of June. It went well, but not how I'd hoped.

"I don't think it would be a good use of time to talk about things that have happened," he began. "The past can be too complicated to get into and it's better to start fresh. My role is to help you figure out how to work out problems as they come up. I also want you to give Nancy a chance to sort all of this out. She's new to the team, to the role, and a new person always shakes up the dynamic a bit especially if it's a new manager. I have faith that she will fix this."

I was disappointed. How could we know how to start over if we didn't understand how we got to where we were? No new issues were arising: the present ones were the same that had been going on for a year. I felt that his comments weren't meant to help me move forward so much as to avoid dealing with the current mess. I also didn't have the confidence in Nancy that he had. She was too new for me to know if she'd have a positive influence and I didn't feel I had the psychological energy to wait for her to catch up.

However, The Boss was supportive in other ways. "Don't let them chase you out," he said. "You have every right to be on that team." It was the most meaningful compliment he had paid me in a long time. Unfortunately, I didn't have the will to fight anymore, and frankly I also wondered if he was sincere: my past experience with him and the Number 2 made me question whether he genuinely valued me or if he simply didn't want the bother of restaffing my position.

Even still, it was nice having this kind of interaction with him. I missed hearing the advice and wisdom he offered from his days as my manager. He offered to mentor me, which I accepted, though I wondered if he was doing it on instruction from The Director. Clearly, enough had happened between us that I no longer had the unwavering faith in him that I used to.

In July it happened: I accepted an offer to join a different division. The Boss was very kind when I told him, saying he knew I didn't want to leave, but acknowledging that the situation within the team had led to it. He added that he knew I wasn't 100% to blame for everything that happened. I wondered what percentage he thought I *was* responsible for.

I told Nancy, who asked if I'd also told Helen. "No, I thought maybe you would like to tell her since you're the manager." I wanted to avoid any conversation with Helen.

"I think it should come from you," Nancy replied.

I wanted to keep my announcement to her as quick and painless as possible, so I told her when she was walking down the hall. Helen acted pleasant and civil and asked whether I'd told Nancy.

"Yes." She looked displeased, then quickly turned around and walked away, as if she was angry for not being told first. The next day she was polite, but also curt and cold. I was grateful that my time with her would end soon.

She retaliated by refusing to let me leave as early as I

wanted. I wanted to leave for my new assignment at the end of August, thinking one month was adequate notice, but Helen wanted to keep me on till the end of September. Nancy agreed with Helen but said I could leave earlier if I completed my tasks ahead of time. I had weekly meetings with Nancy and Helen to update them on how those tasks were progressing and was willing to meet even more if it meant I could leave sooner.

My facilitator from Informal Conflict Management was happy for me. She told me that leaving meant my work life was going to improve and, therefore, I didn't need to meet with her anymore, though I could call on her if I needed her again. I agreed, and thanked her for her pragmatic support and guidance.

My third and final nightmare happened around this time.

I was in a boat floating down a stream, bordered by the same grassy fields in my first nightmare. I approached an intersection at which I could keep going straight or turn left. I looked to my left. In the distance was the same cobblestone bridge I walked over. This time, though, I saw the three bodies hanging from their nooses. I wasn't close enough to see their faces, but knew they were dead. I turned my head to look in front again, feeling nothing about what I just saw, continuing straight down the stream. Then I woke up.

A lunch with friends in August forced me to redefine what had happened over the past year. These friends were from my team, when times had been good. Some of them were still part of it when Erica, Helen, and Sam joined. Their familiarity with the project and the people made it easy for me to explain what was going on.

When I finished, one of them quickly said, "That's workplace violence!"

I felt dumbstruck. I was familiar with the definitions but thought them too vaguely worded to make me sure if what happened to me was serious enough to qualify. My friend, however, had just attended a training session on it and was able to explain it much more concretely. Realizing that my experience could be workplace violence gave me a sense of clarity. What was once a mess of emotions, people, and events could now be packed in a box, tied up, and labelled. Labelling it helped me feel separate from it. *This was because of them, not me.*

It was freeing but, if it was them, then they could target someone else after I left. If there was no written account of what had happened, then it would be partially my fault if that person didn't get the support they needed. So I wanted to leave knowing that my experiences were on record, hoping that management would take more constructive action if history repeated itself. I began writing down the chain of events – episodes of violence – that had occurred since Erica started causing me grief in 2016, including my actions and efforts to address the issues. I even added ideas for trainings and initiatives that the division could implement to improve the team's environment and help everyone on the floor as a whole.

As I worked on this, Helen was preparing her last mid-year review of me.

She downgraded me on a work objective and two personal competencies. The work objective was the discrepancy with

Sam's work. "This would have been avoided had you consulted Sam and been willing to work with him," she said.

"I didn't feel safe around him," I began. "Remember that this is the man who attacked me, never showed any remorse, and attempted to discredit me by going through my work."

"You should have risen above that."

We shifted to competencies. "You are good at what you do, but you don't work well with others. You have problems with everyone you work with," she said.

Wait a minute.

I challenged her. Except for Sam and Erica, I named each person on the team, one by one, asking how I demonstrated having an issue with them. She admitted that I got along with each of them.

"Then the only people I had problems with are Erica and Sam, and the reasons for that are well known. I shouldn't be downgraded for wanting to protect myself against those who attacked me. You should also remember that they refused my offer to use Informal Conflict Management to resolve our differences."

I felt bold and empowered. This was going to be my last evaluation from her. I was also sleeping better. Not more than before, but I had gained better clarity of mind from waking up later – and that clarity came with a set of wits that refused to be suppressed.

"I will take what you said into consideration when I write the final review," Helen coldly replied. Despite winning each of my challenges with Helen, I knew well enough that she might discount anything that opposed what she wanted to believe. If she wanted to vilify me, she would use whatever reason she made up in her head and believe it, too.

I went to Nancy about Helen's evaluation. I explained what Helen's findings were and why I disputed them. Nancy said she would get Helen's side of the story and proceed based on what she found. I didn't get any signal from her that she would 100% side with me, but I felt she would have *had* to at least somewhat. Helen's easily disprovable claim that I had problems with every person on the team would be one thing. I hoped it might be enough for Nancy to question her other comments as well.

My last day with the team was September 15, 2017.

I was going to meet with Nancy and The Director at the end of September about my experiences of workplace violence within the team, though I didn't label it as such to them. I wrote down everything I wanted to say, word for word, and read it back to myself to make sure I didn't go over the allotted meeting time, but also to prevent me from getting lost in emotion and confusion. I'd learned that from my blubbering in front of The Boss back in July.

As I prepared what I wanted to say, I felt that I might need to mention The Boss or that he could come up in conversation. If I were to say anything about him, then I should do him the courtesy of telling him about it first.

"You're not in my speaking points specifically, but some of these experiences do involve you and your name might come up. Is there anything that you don't want me to say or you want me to include?"

"I'm not concerned about anything you might say. I can justify any decision I've made." I couldn't tell if he sounded assertive or arrogant.

When I thought about his answer later, I wondered what

his justification was to let Sam drive me to tears then walk out of the room with him back in March.

At the meeting with Nancy and The Director, I went over what had happened between Erica, Helen, Sam, and myself, the behaviours and interpersonal dynamics I observed within the team that I felt contributed to that, and suggestions for what I thought we could do organizationally to prevent these situations or help employees going through them. Nancy and The Director did not interrupt me and appeared to listen with interest. I thought everything went well – till the end. I offered The Director the paper with my script as written documentation of workplace violence, but she refused to accept it. I couldn't understand why. I returned to my desk, in my new job, and wondered if I would ever return to where I had called home for seven years.

SNAKES

ENTERING THE PIT

INSOMNIA IS, FOR me, both self-feeding and self-consuming.

It starts with a half-asleep morning of imaginary conversations in the hopes that one will answer the unresolved questions in your head. You wake up having forgotten the conversations, but not the emotions they generated. You go to work carrying those emotions with you. And for each failed attempt you make during the day to answer those questions, your brain has more hurt, anger, and confusion to feed upon. You then wake up the next morning, possibly earlier than before, dealing with that.

Then come the attacks from those who smelled your blood in the water. Now your head is dealing with the resulting fear and anxiety. You see evidence of subterfuge around you and now your brain wakes up imagining what else might be happening. You go into work primed to defend yourself against more attacks. If you don't, you'll get blindsided again. You always need to be ready to spot the attack when it's happening and be prepared with a response so they don't bring you down.

But because you know you're primed and haven't slept, you ask yourself whether what you're seeing is innocent, more subterfuge, or more of the violence you already experienced. You constantly question your judgment, your interpretations, and the justification for how it makes you feel. And so your brain wakes up earlier to sort all of that out, on top of everything else that remains unresolved. The cycle continues.

The insomnia, begun by unresolved hurt, anger, confusion, and anxiety, gets continuously fed by more of the same as you see and hear things that generate those emotions, all while you're wondering if the insomnia that this caused is leading you to more of it, slowly driving you insane.

In October, Nancy scheduled a meeting to go over my official mid-year review. I was pleasantly surprised that she would be discussing it with me instead of Helen, whom I was glad not to see again. Nancy had been kind to me in our short time working together. I felt understood when she listened to my concerns about Sam, and appreciated how she had agreed to let me leave the team early if I completed my deliverables. But I also remembered Helen's imagination and her treating assumptions as facts. What had Helen told Nancy and did Nancy believe it? So, it was with some trepidation that I walked into that meeting room.

My trepidation proved to be justified. "I consulted Helen and chose to agree with her assessment of you. The discrepancy you caused, which was avoidable, took a lot of time to resolve, causing delays in the project."

"I offered to go back to Sam's method. If we had done that, the problem would have been resolved earlier."

"Still, you need to be held responsible for it happening in the first place. As for your competencies, I agree with Helen that you don't work well with others on the team. Your refusal to work with Sam demonstrates that because, if you had been willing to work with him, you would have consulted him about your methodology and avoided this problem altogether or been able to resolve it with him."

Wait a minute.

"I don't understand that," I said. "Remember that Sam bullied me earlier this year and never showed any sign of wanting to work that out with me, and you said yourself more could have been done to resolve that situation. Also, the opinion that I don't get along with my co-workers is coming from someone who yelled at me in my last mid-year review and you've seen me get along well with everyone else on the team. How can you believe everything in her review so easily when you've seen for yourself that at least that part isn't true?"

Nancy wouldn't address my challenge directly, saying only, "I will make sure it is mentioned in your review that you weren't the only one responsible for the issues between you and Sam."

The certainty in Nancy's voice told me that she would not be swayed. If I continued to argue it could be mentioned in my review as another reason to downgrade me. Nancy's presentation was entirely verbal, and so I thought it was best not to react till I saw the actual written wording. I was in shock that she sided with Helen so fully, but I kept everything amicable and thanked her for taking the time to explain the review to me.

I took a walk outside at lunch, alone, feeling defeated.

The official, written review was sent to me the next day. Helen followed Nancy's instruction to note that I wasn't solely responsible for the issues on the team, but it was literally one short line tacked on at the end of a paragraph that was still full of falsehoods. As for my work objectives, all the good that I accomplished in those six months was summarized in a few lines, whereas there were three paragraphs about the discrepancies. Nancy told me that if I still disagreed with any aspect of my review, I could add a comment before signing off. I just couldn't do that. I couldn't sign off on all the lies Helen had written about me in the competencies or on how one mistake took up three-quarters of the text in that section.

I was grateful to be elsewhere in the agency at this point. In the short time I had been there, I had developed a good rapport with my supervisors. My new manager was completely uninvolved with my old team, so I felt I could trust her to provide some neutral advice. She advised me to contact the union.

I told the union representative about the review and my experiences with Helen. He advised that I could file a grievance, adding that Helen's yelling at me could be interpreted as workplace violence, but suggested trying to resolve it amicably first. In the meantime, I should add a comment in the employee section of the review expressing my disagreement and the reasons why. I did so, giving my own perspective on what had happened, correcting Helen's incorrect assumptions, and providing examples where I demonstrated the competencies she had said I lacked. Then, with the union's guidance, I emailed Nancy and The Director asking to meet to discuss why I was not prepared to sign the review. They didn't answer. I was so upset by all of this. I was gone: why couldn't they let me leave in peace?

Leaving the project, and the floor I was on, gave me the psychological space I needed to separate from all of this and regain some of my strength. I was still trancing and waking up early, but not being among the people who caused it helped me feel freer than I had felt in a long time. Instead, the fact that Nancy and The Director never answered my request encouraged me to fight. It told me that they weren't interested in helping me. The only one left to fight for me now was me, and my new independence felt empowering. The union sent me links about harassment and workplace violence. I looked at them all, trying to absorb as much as I could.

The next step was the union going through Labour Relations to see if my concerns could be resolved informally. If they couldn't be, then we could grieve the review. Helen and Nancy not only refused Labour Relations' request, they added that they were refusing because I had "cut communication with the unit." The union rep and I took that to mean that Helen and Nancy accused me of having stopped speaking to every person the team. I couldn't believe that they would lie like that. There were two employees whom I spoke to daily, other team members I was friendly with – and Nancy, who sat next to me on the other side of my cubicle wall, saw it all. Not to mention my weekly meetings with her and Helen before I left. I could see this coming from Helen, but not her. The rep told me that the answer came from Nancy.

I felt even more encouraged to file the grievance, but worried that it would be waging war against Helen and Nancy, encouraging them to tell more lies and make more false assumptions about me. What if The Director, the first person to whom the grievance would go, sided with them? My interactions with The Director had left me feeling that I could trust her, but I had once felt that way about Nancy, too.

And I hadn't forgotten how The Director didn't respond to my meeting request. Was The Director going to betray me next?

Ultimately, I couldn't let Helen's and Nancy's lies about me go unanswered. The union prepared an official grievance application and statement. I submitted it to Helen on November 25, 2017.

In the lead-up to the grievance hearing, I found myself sinking into cynicism about human nature, the value of interpersonal relationships at work, and my professional future at the agency. My trances became more frequent. I was imagining how the hearing would go and what might be said, how my character might be attacked, and maybe needing to escalate my grievance to the highest authority for any chance of redress. I knew that all of this negativity was doing me in, but I felt powerless to stop it.

Reading and submitting the grievance were what set me off. It included details of how I was harmed by Sam and Helen and what I was seeking to be "made whole," a term meaning "this is what it will take for me to feel that this situation was fairly and adequately addressed." The violent history with Helen was outside the scope of the grievance because it had happened the previous year, but it could be mentioned because it showed the history of violence and, therefore, framed her judgments of me in a different light.

There was something about reading it all in black and white that made me relive it a little. It concretized what was about to happen. I was scared to face the unknown reality that was headed my way, and my trances were trying to mitigate that by preparing me for every possible negative turn that could happen. What I needed was someone to tell me what The Director was thinking and where I stood with her. I was so tired at this point of wondering whether I was valued by those I looked up to, of suspecting that I was being targeted in malicious conversations, and of worrying over who thought what about me. I wanted so much to be positive, relaxed, and for someone, a disinterested someone, to simply tell me what to think.

I felt my chest tighten and my mind race heading into the hearing, despite the union rep having walked me through what to expect. It took a while to calm myself down.

Fortunately, the hearing went smoothly. There were no accusations, nor any character assassinations. The Director asked questions about the grievance, looked at us when we spoke, nodded to acknowledge that she heard our arguments, took notes and asked questions about points that she was unsure about. She always looked and sounded kind. Her only surprising comment was when the union rep labelled Sam's behaviour as workplace violence, saying that it was news to her. I didn't understand whether she was pretending she didn't know about what happened or whether she was surprised by the label. I didn't challenge her because I feared doing so would make me look argumentative or that she might turn against me. So I told myself that she claimed ignorance because she wanted to look good in front of Labour Relations. I didn't want to believe otherwise.

The union rep and I agreed that the meeting had gone smoothly, and I felt encouraged by The Director's receptiveness. However, I knew I wouldn't know anything till I saw the judgment document. All I could do now was wait.

SLITHERING UP THE GASLIGHT

GASLIGHTING: THE PROCESS of making somebody believe untrue things in order to control them, especially that they have imagined or been wrong about what has really happened. – Oxford Learner's Dictionaries

When I joined my new team, I made a conscious decision not to look at them through the same lens that I had learned to see my former colleagues through. None of them had ever worked with me or on that project before, I'd never heard any of their names through the grapevine, and nor had they likely ever heard mine. Therefore, they did not deserve to have my previous experiences influence how they were seen or spoken to. This meant being constantly mindful of my history and of how I was perceiving their words and actions, and intentionally choosing to build relationships with them.

Thanks to this decision, I found myself surrounded by colleagues who acted respectfully towards each other, helped when needed, thanked those who helped them, and pulled their own weight to get the job done. I also had a manager who valued mental health in the workplace, which she showed by being candid about her own mental health challenges and how that influenced her to prioritize well-being for herself and her team. Both she and my direct supervisor knew I had come from a very difficult experience. They made it clear I could go to them for support, and I believed them because of the respect I saw them demonstrate to each other and everyone else. They and the rest of the team were exactly the type of people I needed around me at that time. I felt hopeful that the last three years would one day be a small blip in my career instead of a dominant part of it.

Being in a supportive environment helped me sleep more peacefully, which led to reclaiming more of my strength and self-confidence. I started recognizing that I had made good professional and personal choices while with my former team: I sought advice on how to address mental health issues for the team and proposed initiatives to management, showed patience and kindness when I chose to give Erica the benefit of the doubt when my conflict with her first began, tried to resolve my conflict with Sam immediately after it happened and sought help when I couldn't, and sought and implemented advice on how to confront my anxiety around Helen. And the fact that I developed and maintained positive relationships with other people on the team, elsewhere on the floor, and with people in my new work unit were all evidence that I could work well with others. As for the discrepancies Sam found, the fact that this was the only glaring error mentioned in any review of mine during the seven years I spent on that team meant I still knew how to do my job well.

2018

While awaiting the decision on my grievance, I chose to keep rebuilding my relationship with The Boss. My new job was a one-year assignment. I could ask to remain there permanently, but The Director could also pull me back saying that "operational needs" required me to return. And despite the last three years I spent on that team, there were still four good years before it and relationships with people who were still there. I wanted to know if there was any potential to return and be happy, and having a good relationship again with The Boss needed to be part of that. I needed to know that there would be someone in my proverbial corner should anything go awry again. He wasn't involved in the grievance and I didn't know if he even knew about it.

So, on a random day in January, I decided I would pay him an unannounced visit, just to say hello. I took the elevator up. As soon as I reached the floor, I froze. All the confidence I had when I entered the elevator left me and I was instantly paralyzed by a wave of anxiety. The doors opened, but I couldn't leave. I stood frozen, in the corner, both hands clutching the railing behind me, praying that no one would walk by and see me. After what felt like several minutes, the doors closed and the elevator went back down again. I exhaled one heavy breath, and relaxed enough to let go of the railing. To this day, I don't know why I reacted this way. When I returned to my desk, I emailed The Boss asking if he'd like to meet, and he agreed to meet for coffee later that week.

The Director made her decision about the grievance in March. Normally, this would be shared in a formal meeting between her, representatives from Labour Relations and the union, and me. However, my union rep was going to be out of town, so I was offered the option to meet with The Director informally, no union or Labour Relations reps present. I agreed because I was anxious to know what she had decided. I also felt confident that a private conversation would go smoothly, even if her decision didn't go my way.

It began well. She agreed to overturn Helen's competency ratings and put me back on track. She said that she had seen enough of me during my time under her to know that Helen's comments did not reflect who I was. I was thankful that she recognized that. However, in exchange for erasing Helen's comments about me, she wanted me to erase mine. I felt this was a fair exchange, and agreed.

Unfortunately, The Director was going to maintain the "needs improvement" ranking for my work objectives. She agreed with Helen that I should have found the discrepancies and corrected them earlier. I was disappointed, but knew she was right. However, The Director recognized that using three-quarters of the space to write about it while covering every other accomplishment only briefly was misleading. She would tell Helen to soften the wording.

I agreed to withdraw the grievance in exchange for the changes she promised. The meeting had gone as well as I thought it could and she was as kind and respectful as I'd expected her to be. I thanked her for her time and for restoring my competency ratings, and she wished me well in return.

But then, as I reached for the door to leave her office, she said, "We'll meet again soon because there are other things I want to talk to you about."

I stopped. "What did you want to talk about?"

"I'll let you know when we meet," she answered.

"Can I know now?"

"No, don't worry about it. We'll talk about it when the time comes."

I was feeling increasingly anxious. She seemed to be trying hard not to tell me what was up. "I would like to at least have an idea now," I countered. "If I don't, I'm going to be waking up early every morning wondering what this will be about."

She looked at me and reluctantly said, "I want to talk to you about what happened between you and your previous supervisor." She was referring to the Number 2.

I immediately felt defensive. As far as I knew, those issues were resolved when he left the team two years prior. "Why do you want to talk about him?" I asked.

"We'll go into that when we meet," she answered.

Why was she being so coy? "We can talk about it later, but remember that this ended years ago and I wasn't the only one who had had a problem with him." The Director waved me back into her guest chair, probably sensing that I was enough on edge that this conversation couldn't wait. Once I sat down, she told me that she wanted to talk about how I had handled myself.

I didn't know where this conversation was going to go, but my gut told me that I should be ready to defend myself. I had a decision to make: a lot of how I chose to handle the situation had to do with The Boss, but I didn't want to jeopardize rebuilding our relationship by looking like I was badmouthing him behind his back with his superior. However, he had said he didn't regret any of his choices and could defend every single one. *Fine*, I thought. *Let him defend himself.*

The Director said, "I heard about the issues you had with him and, yes, I know you weren't the only one who did, but how you handled yourself showed that you don't deal with interpersonal difficulties very well. It happened again when you stopped speaking to Sam. This tells me that you don't have the competencies to move up to the next level."

That was a blow. Didn't she understand all the work I had put into the project, the issues I had dealt with regarding the Number 2, Louise, Erica, Helen, and Sam, and the suggestions I'd made to try to improve everything? What about the positive relationships I had with so many other people, which she acknowledged when she agreed to overturn my poor competency ratings? Did none of this count for anything?

Regardless, the situations with the Number 2 and with Sam were completely different. "I don't think these are comparable," I answered. "First, what happened with Sam was labelled workplace violence."

"I don't think Sam treated you as badly as you say he did," she answered. Then, referring to The Boss, "He briefed me on what happened. He said that everything Sam said could be said in ten minutes."

"The meeting lasted nearly an hour," I countered.

She did not acknowledge this, instead continuing, "I don't think Sam was trying to upset you. You should understand that he reacted that way because he felt ambushed, which you caused by asking for help. And I don't think Sam was trying to discredit you when he found and reported the discrepancies in your work; he had only the project's best interests in mind when he did that. You should have also felt safe in your environment and known that Nancy would protect you, and been more engaged in your meetings with Sam."

Wow.

"First, I shouldn't be blamed for ambushing Sam when

it was his idea to handle it that way," I countered, referring to The Boss. "And Sam attacked me in that meeting to the point where he drove me to tears. I had to leave the room to get a hold of myself and, when I came back, he picked up right where he left off. If he wasn't trying to hurt me, then he would have stopped or stepped back when he saw how upset I became. The fact that he didn't shows *intent*. As for Nancy, she lied when she said I 'cut communication with the unit.' The fact that she would lie to Labour Relations so blatantly shows that I was right not to have faith in her."

The Director stared silently at me for a moment. She then began a story about a boss she once had who would yell at her and her assistant about their work. "My assistant would leave those meetings spitting mad, but it never bothered me that much and I told him to let it go. I would just redo the work the way my boss wanted and move on. You need to learn not to take things so personally."

So how they treated me wasn't the problem; my reaction was?

The Director said she knew I had issues with The Boss. "I don't know what they were, but your body language showed it. There are meetings where I saw you sitting with your chair turned away from him or looking at everyone but him in the room when you talked. This also tells me that you don't handle interpersonal difficulties well."

I was shocked by how much she had perceived. "Yes, there were issues," I replied, "And I tried to sort them out with him multiple times, but he refused."

The Director ignored this and replied, "But you didn't show any effort to do so with your co-workers."

"I did. I made an effort when I attended a mental health seminar and suggested that the team create a code of conduct, offered to do Informal Conflict Management sessions with Sam and Erica to resolve our differences, and talked to Helen about bringing in a facilitator to work with the team. Those efforts failed because my co-workers refused them all."

Without skipping a beat, The Director said, "You can't expect people to cooperate."

So, first I'm being criticized for not doing enough, and then for having tried?

The Director also raised my earlier silence towards Erica. "It was Erica who originally wanted that and agreed to it when I offered it later," I answered, continuing by going over the dynamic I observed between Erica and Helen over those same months and Helen's one-sidedness during that whole time.

I was being blamed not only for my choices, but for others' as well. I looked straight at The Director and said, "No one forced them to yell at me on the street, over the table, or dig through my work to discredit me. I will take responsibility for my choices but I won't take responsibility for theirs." The Director looked at me, wide-eyed and silent, as if she were shocked to have heard that.

The meeting ended after I asked her whether The Boss had offered to mentor me because she'd asked him to or if it was something he genuinely wanted to do. She said it was the latter, but agreed to follow up with him.

I walked away feeling disappointed that The Director didn't appreciate how serious and damaging the last few years' events had been for me.

I realized the next day that I never asked her whether she had addressed the workplace violence allegations from the grievance. I wasn't optimistic but I knew this would bother me till I had a firm answer. The Director agreed to a half-hour meeting in her office.

I first asked about what she did, if anything, about what I told her and Nancy during that meeting in September. The Director immediately became agitated and defensive, turning the question back on me. "You said a lot that day. You can't expect Nancy and me to remember all of it."

"I know I said a lot, and that's why I offered you my notes. You could have taken them."

The Director looked flustered. "Nancy and I gave you the time you needed to say what you wanted to say. I assure you that you were *heard*."

Not *acknowledged*, not *listened to*, not *taken seriously*. Just *heard*. I felt that was her way of saying that everything I'd shared had been ignored.

"Did you ever speak with Sam or Helen about my allegations in the grievance?" I asked.

"I investigated Sam. I had to because he was mentioned in the grievance."

Had to? So, The Director didn't look into how Helen treated me because the grievance didn't *make* her? Now I knew that The Director had ignored my allegations, either because she didn't believe me or wanted to silence me. I knew from her agitated posture that I wasn't going to get anywhere by continuing this topic, so I dropped it and asked her the other question I came with: was I welcome back in the division?

"You are absolutely welcome back," she answered cheerily. "You're an asset here." Then she listed three teams and managers that she could place me in: a manager whose team didn't have any openings; the Number 2, who had since returned to the agency and now managed his own team; or my same former team. The fact that she offered two teams with people I had problems with made me wonder if she only wanted it to look like she wanted me back but discourage me by making the options so unpalatable.

"I'm surprised you're suggesting my old team after how they treated me. I doubt they want me back either."

"Nonsense," she replied. "They would love to have you back." This was probably the most disingenuous statement from her in this whole process, and the final thing I needed to hear to know that I couldn't take her seriously. My disappointment from the day before turned into anger at her for not investigating my claims. I was incredulous.

I vented about all of this to my psychologist. I told her that the constant flurry of ever-changing emotions was taking its toll on me and I longed for inner calm. She handed me a list of things I could do to distract myself.

A few days later, I told the union rep what The Director had said about investigating the allegations. He was disappointed and told me I had two options: speak to an anti-harassment officer and request an investigation into what occurred, with corrective measures that could be mandated and enforced; or have a "competent, neutral third party" come in to investigate by interviewing each person involved and then make recommendations at the departmental level to ensure that what happened to me didn't happen again. I would need The Director's approval for the second option and didn't think I would get it. I knew that requesting an investigation would nail the door shut for good on going back and I wasn't ready for that.

I spent a lot of time ruminating over The Director's comments while waiting for my revised review to come in. I was struck by how often she tried to play both sides, making a contradictory argument when I'd prove the first one wrong, or blame me for what happened. In her mind, the problem wasn't how other people treated me, but rather how I couldn't accept and work with it. And the fact that she brought up the Number 2, a situation that had been dead for the last two years (or so I thought), told me that I would never escape the past. As for everything else, she dismissed what she could and minimized the rest.

I struggled to reconcile how the person who appeared so kind and supportive at the beginning could then pin so much of what happened onto me. After much thought, I concluded that the kindness and empathy I saw before was nothing more than superficial compassion expressed with the appropriate buzzwords. I felt lucky to be working elsewhere. I could see myself clinging to whatever threads of hope and validation I could find if I were still on my former floor, my judgment clouded from being so physically close to the situation, improved sleep or not. But now in a psychologically healthier environment, I was benefitting from my improved sleep even more. I was able to think more rationally, and being around people who behaved with kindness and respect reminded me of how teams could and should function. These helped me see both the toxicity within my old environment and how the management structure above enabled it.

I received the revised review. My competency ratings were what The Director had promised. The negativity in my work rating was condensed but still longer than my accomplishments, however I knew that this was the best I could expect from Helen. I was disappointed that The Director accepted such minimal changes and wondered whether she did so as payback for me challenging her. Nevertheless, I didn't think I'd get better by escalating it, so I signed off on the revised review and withdrew the grievance.

But the fact that The Director never truly investigated my allegations continued to bother me and I felt like I was getting this improved review in exchange for my silence about what happened. I didn't want to support that. So, I reneged on my promise to remove my comments, instead modifying them to mention the workplace violence that happened. The Director sent a second email with a link to mentorship resources and wished me success in finding a good match. I interpreted that to mean that The Boss hadn't offered to mentor me freely.

The Director emailed me about my comments, including people in the cc whom I didn't know. She wrote that it wasn't until the grievance hearing that she heard about the allegation of workplace violence. She included links to EAP, Informal Conflict Management, and other resources that she suggested I contact to help me deal with the aftereffects. She also suggested that I contact one of the agency's Integrity and Respect Officers if I wanted to discuss my allegations with someone who was trained in harassment and violence.

I saw her email as a butt-covering exercise. I wondered whether me calling it workplace violence somehow escalated how seriously she had to take it and so she needed to defend why she hadn't done anything. The Director thus became another person I couldn't trust or rely on for support. I couldn't let her deception go unchallenged, but my response had to be carefully worded. I couldn't be emotional or argumentative, but I needed to be believable in a way that trumped the credibility she possessed due to her rank. This was what I wrote:

I am writing because I am concerned about the comment you made that the grievance hearing was the first time you were made aware of the workplace violence. I recall you saying this when we last met but, now that this has been repeated in writing, I feel required to respond.

First, I believe we can agree that the grievance hearing was not the first time you heard about what occurred with Sam. We discussed it last spring, at which point you told me that The Boss had already informed you of it, and I raised it during my exit interview in September, all prior to the hearing in December. Further, considering that this incident impacted my working relationship with Sam, and that impact was used to justify Helen's comments on my ability to work with others, it should not have been surprising that the incident was raised during the hearing.

Perhaps the issue is that the hearing was, at least to my knowledge, the first time this incident was labelled as *workplace violence*. This was not done to shock or surprise. I had not applied the label earlier as even I was not fully aware that what occurred with Sam (and even more so with Helen) fit its definition. I came to learn this over the course of the grievance process via my conversations with the union. After the hearing, this learning was reinforced through the online corporate training on workplace violence and its in-class counterpart on the Occupational Health and Safety Act. It is unfortunate that this education did not come earlier, but its timing should not affect how we identify what occurred within the team.

From our conversations, it appears to me that we do not

agree on how to define *workplace violence* nor on the severity of what occurred within the team. I am disappointed by
that and, regretfully, do not know how to bridge this gap nor
whether such bridging is possible.

Nevertheless, let me close by thanking you for sending the
links to the pages on harassment and the list of Integrity and
Respect Officers, as well as for your earlier links to mentorship resources within and outside the agency. I am uncertain
which path to pursue, if any, but I assure you that any decision I make will be an informed one.

I felt so angry at The Director's and The Boss's unwillingness to
address, let alone acknowledge, what had happened. I was angry
more so at The Director because she was the one who'd told me
I needed to show that I was willing to work with others to fix
this – yet not expect my efforts to succeed, while she then did
nothing. Anger, hurt, anxiety, and disappointment had become
such a constant presence that I almost couldn't remember what
it felt like to feel carefree and happy.

I decided to speak with an Integrity and Respect Officer.
I chose the one who used to manage the agency's Occupational Health and Safety program and run the harassment and
workplace violence workshop. *Perfect*, I thought. *If anyone on
this list would know if this was violence and take me seriously, it
would be her*. I emailed her to arrange a meeting.

GETTING BIT

I PLANNED TO keep my story brief and at a high level with the Integrity and Respect Officer. The Officer was another Director, so I knew she was busy and I didn't want to take up more of her time than necessary, let alone appear over-emotional or didn't know when to stop talking. So I focused on what happened with Helen and Sam, plus the insomnia and anxiety attacks. I felt incredibly dishonest not including Erica and all that happened with her, but I didn't want that to cloud over everything else.

The Integrity and Respect Officer worked in a different building than mine, which helped me feel more comfortable, less watched. She welcomed me warmly into her office with a gentle smile and an empathetic tone. Her role, she said, was to listen, be neutral, and guide me to appropriate resources if needed. She then introduced her colleague, the new manager of the agency's Occupational Health and Safety program, who joined us to explain what harassment and workplace violence were, their differences and overlaps, and the fact that only a trained evaluator could determine under which of them a person's experiences fell, if either. He then left and the officer invited me to tell my story.

The officer told me that my experiences definitely fell under the umbrella of harassment and workplace violence and she would consult someone in Labour Relations to find out how to guide me. She acknowledged that these types of experiences can "scar" people and it would be natural if I felt that way. I had never heard the impact described as scars before: it felt apt. She put me in touch with someone in Labour Relations and advised me to reach out to EAP or Informal Conflict Management.

I reached out to my former facilitator from Informal Conflict Management and got to see her the next day. She and I talked about how I was happy and peaceful in my new work environment, but the former situation hung over me darkly and inescapably, the negative feelings all coming back every time I was reminded of what happened or saw someone who was involved. I finished by telling her how I was debating whether to pursue an investigation. The facilitator asked me to consider this: where do I draw the line? When do I say that I did what I set out to do, and then let it go? I'd never thought about that. Her pragmatism was a much-needed wind gust into my brain, ridding it of cobwebs and leaving a fresh atmosphere behind.

It was now May. I met with a woman from Labour Relations, assuming that the meeting would be more formal – documented and with actions arising – because they have somewhat of an enforcement role in the agency. I decided I would be open about everything that happened, including Erica. I began by saying that I stopped speaking to an employee for some weeks –

"That's harassment," she interrupted.

I was stunned into silence. Not by what she said, but by how abruptly she cut me off and how definitively she made her judgment. I paused to catch my breath and regroup my thoughts. I started again, "Perhaps there are circumstances – "

"No," she cut in. "Not speaking to an employee is harassment and the circumstances don't matter."

I felt I had lost my argument before I could make it, overpowered by her assertiveness and firmness. I moved on to Sam and Helen, explaining the major events, the grievance, and the fact that The Director had not even spoken to Sam about my allegations.

"I'm surprised to hear that," she said, referring to The Director's inaction, and then looked down to scribble something quickly in her notebook.

She also backed up the Integrity and Respect Officer's conclusion that their actions could be considered harassment or workplace violence. "You can do one of two things," she said. "Have faith that The Director had resolved everything, or file a formal complaint and request an investigation through the *Canada Labour Code*." I hated both options. They were either "go big or go home." No middle ground.

"What is the name of your director?" she asked, and scribbled it in her notebook after I told her.

"Did you want the names of those whose acts I talked about?"

"No, I only need the name of the director." I found it odd that she didn't want to know who had actually committed the violence. Would The Director get the blame for others' actions? Would she corroborate my account of events? I left the meeting feeling very unsure of what to expect next.

I later confirmed with my union rep that the two options were really all that were available to me, adding that if an investigation came back unfounded, then those whom I'd filed the complaint against could then file one against me. I didn't fear that as I didn't think they'd have grounds to win one. However, with two years now having passed since everything had begun with Erica, I had to ask myself whether an investigation would be worthwhile. Any one of the people who hurt me could say that they didn't remember what happened, or lie outright. I didn't have any evidence – no emails, no neutral witnesses – to prove any of my claims. It would be entirely my word against theirs.

I was emotionally exhausted. All the negative feelings had taken their toll on me and I didn't have the energy to keep pushing. None of this was resolved, I wasn't satisfied, but I felt I had gone as far as I could go. All I wanted now was emotional peace, and I wouldn't get that if I kept living with everything that had happened. And so I decided to forego an investigation and leave my old division permanently.

I continued mourning the loss of The Director's support that I thought I had, but other, more positive feelings also began to develop. Since joining a much healthier team, I didn't have to contend with being constantly surrounded by toxicity, history, or being reminded by others of what was wrong with me. That, plus having a new job to learn, helped me to detach somewhat from what had happened, opening my eyes to what I had going for me. My accomplishments, skills, and aptitudes were seen as strengths instead of points to be used in self-defence. The "I'm not as bad as you think because … " became "I'm a leader who's good at what I do and this is why."

I felt that if I didn't share this with The Director, I would be allowing her to keep believing what she did about me and, possibly, letting her think that I believed it myself. My pride wouldn't allow that. I knew that I might not convert her to my way of thinking, but I knew doing nothing wouldn't convert her either. I had very little to lose and could at least say I tried. I had had more successes than failures there and deserved better than to have those successes dismissed.

So I wrote her a letter that included what I'd learned about how my experiences were viewed by the Integrity and Respect Officer, Labour Relations, and the union. I wrote that they all had said that Helen's and Sam's actions against me could be harassment or workplace violence, and they explained to me that I could return to the division, or not, or request an investigation.

I wrote that I did not believe she had ever addressed any of the issues, listing comments she had made in our meeting and her earlier refusal to take my speaking notes as evidence. Then I argued why I was ready to be promoted. I had not only the skills and experience, I wrote, but also had had my competencies challenged in a way most employees never do. I asked her to consider, out of all the people she thought ready for promotion, if any of them ever had to deal directly with workplace violence or harassment, let alone suggest ideas to help address mental health issues or team behaviour. The fact that I did those things while simultaneously dealing with the psychological impact of what was happening to me made me a strong individual who could lead. To tell me that I was still lacking minimized the impact the environment had on me, dismissed what I'd tried to do, and imposed expectations on me that others never had to meet. I asked her to respond if I'd misunderstood anything.

I concluded by asking her to approve extending my stay in my new team till the end of the fiscal year. It saddened me to ask for that because I considered my old team to be my home for seven years but, I wrote, it was not in my interest to return. Once I sent that letter, a wave of calm washed over me. The Director approved my request to extend my assignment.

Later in June a posting came out for the promotion I wanted. In order to be considered, your past two years of evaluations had to show that you constantly met your work objectives and demonstrated good personal competencies, like initiative and good judgment. So in order to qualify, I would have had to be granted an exemption from that requirement because of the mid-year evaluation from the year before. Directors had the power to grant them. I didn't believe that she would help me, but knew I would regret not trying to convince her. Now I was going to find out whether my letter had any effect.

The promotion meant more to me than a pay raise or more advanced responsibilities: it meant validation. It would be a sign that senior management truly agreed that what had happened was harassment or violence, that they recognized I had worked hard and that my successes outweighed my failures.

I submitted my application along with my two previous years' performance reviews, with which I included my exemption request. My brain went back to its early-morning ruminations while waiting for an answer.

I bumped into The Director a couple of times while waiting for her decision. The first time was when I was exiting an elevator that she was entering. As soon as she saw me, she stopped in her tracks and turned her head to speak to someone at the other end of the elevator lobby, pretending not to notice that I was right in front of her. I was fine with that. I kept facing forward and walking down the hall.

The second time was in the basement elevator lobby. I was speaking to a former co-worker, me on one side of the lobby and her on the other. Suddenly, out of the corner of my eye, I saw The Director. She exited an elevator and walked right past me, her cell held up high in front of her face so she could see straight down the hall, pretending to look at the phone and not to notice me. My co-worker, who also knew The Director, said hello to her and asked how she was. The Director replied hello and that she was fine, but without looking at my colleague and maintaining her brisk walk pace. I remembered how she criticized me for avoiding interacting with The Boss when I was angry at him three years prior. I wondered whether she was acting this way because she thought it was acceptable for *her* to behave that way but not me, or if it was a tit-for-tat about The Boss.

As time passed and I continued to wait, I felt myself detach more and more from my former work area. I still ruminated early over what I did and didn't know, but I began veering towards how I could make my new assignment permanent and get away from The Director altogether. As long as her division was listed as the one I belonged to, she had the power to decide whether I could stay where I was or return, as well as get promoted. I was anxious over the power that she had over my career. From what I saw, the management in my new area liked me more than The Director did, and so I wanted to be under their power sooner rather than later.

This anxiety affected how I moved about the building as well. Each time I thought of walking the halls or getting a bite to eat, I feared running into The Director or The Boss. I felt that they believed their rank and relationship to me obliged me to happily say hello to them if I passed them in the hall or to make small talk with them in the elevator. I didn't want to. I wanted to forget them, and I wanted them to forget me. So I took every measure I could to avoid running into them. I worked on the third floor, so I'd take the stairs up to my floor instead of the elevator, avoid the cafeteria during peak times, or pick a floor in the adjacent building that they had no reason to be on for my lunchtime walk when the weather was bad. I felt at peace when I knew I wouldn't see them.

In November, I learned that my exemption request was denied, but by the staffing committee and not The Director. With my union rep's help, we spoke to someone in Human Resources who told us that my request had gone to The Director, but she'd refused to make the decision and instead passed it back to the committee. I was disappointed that she had had an opportunity to help but chose not to. She didn't even accept the responsibility of choosing. It was obvious that her claim that I was an asset and welcome back had been insincere.

But then she also tried, in my opinion, to blackball me. I learned of this from my new manager after I told her that the exemption hadn't been granted. She replied, "I know. I found out from my boss."

"How does *he* know about this?" I asked.

"Promise me that this stays between us. You're not supposed to know about this. He called me into his office to tell me that she called him," she said, referring to The Director.

"She asked him how you were doing here. He said he hadn't heard anything bad. Then, she told him about your exemption request, that it failed, and that he should keep an eye on you because you have mental health issues. He told me about this because he wanted to know if any of it was true. I told him there was nothing to worry about and that you were working out well here."

I was grateful to her for defending me, but … *wow*.

If The Director made that call a year ago when I left, when I truly was in a bad state, I might have understood why she said that. But now, more than a year later and after the grievance and all the officials I spoke to, I saw this phone call as retaliation. It all reeked to me of the whisper campaigns girls use in high school to ruin someone's reputation. The only reason I didn't report this to the union was because my manager told me that if it got out that I knew, it'd be known that she told me. I liked my new manager, so I kept quiet.

2019

I had been away from Erica, Sam, Helen, and Nancy long enough to no longer feel anxious around them; I knew I could walk by and feel no obligation to acknowledge them. There were no undealt-with emotions towards them. But my anxiety over running into The Director or The Boss remained.

In January, I was in the elevator with a friend, chatting away with my back towards the door. When we stopped on the main floor to let people on, my friend waved to someone who got on who, judging by her reaction, didn't wave back. Curious to know who it was, I looked at their reflection in the mirrored wall that I faced and saw that it was The Boss. He stuck himself into the corner behind me where I wouldn't see him. I don't know why he didn't acknowledge my friend nor say anything to me, but the fact that he didn't felt liberating. It was like a message saying I could cut all ties. If he could ignore me, then I could ignore him, too.

In February, the papers came in making me a permanent employee of my adopted team. I signed them happily, and with relief that I was now no longer under The Director. Later in the year, I learned how fortunate I was to get away: The Director promoted Erica to the same level as me and renewed Helen's two-year assignment with the team. In my mind, this was beyond not taking workplace violence seriously: this was rewarding it. And for Erica to be promoted, she would have had to have clean performance evaluations or been granted an exemption for them, and so she likely had never been disciplined. I had been scapegoated.

The Director moved on to another area in August and The Boss was promoted to replace her. One of the first staffing decisions he made was to give Sam an acting promotion. I too was awarded an acting promotion in January 2020. It was clear that my new management valued me in a way that the old one never did.

I had stopped writing in my journal in April 2019. I still felt the anxiety and I still tranced, but I accepted them as part of me. I knew I couldn't just will them away, so I became at peace with them, letting them happen instead of lamenting over how they were still there. Over those four years, I went from being a cool-headed person to someone who got nervous over who she might run into in the hall. I wanted that cool-headed person back.

I work in a different agency today and have the COVID pandemic to thank for that. Closing the offices and having to work from home helped me start detaching from the agency: I didn't hear rumours or news about my old team or the people I worked with; I didn't feel any anxiety over who I would see in the hall; and, I no longer saw people every day, consequently feeling less like part of a team. As for my job specifically, my acting assignment expired in January 2021 and my job was finished, so I wasn't being promoted permanently. There were also structural and workload shifts in the agency that changed the kind of future I saw available to me there. The moment I moved on, the huge black cloud that had been swirling over my head disappeared. All the people who impacted me then, and could have impacted me again had I stayed, now no longer could. I was free. And that cool-headed person I longed to become again finally came back. I was me again, albeit an older and wiser version, and it's a contentment that stays with me today.

LESSONS LEARNED

MOVING FORWARD

THERE IS LITTLE purpose to experiencing hardships if they cannot be learned from or used for good.

Even before the events in this book, I was someone who believed that there is a reason behind whatever we're experiencing or whoever we're with. The wonderful or horrible thing we just went through was for a purpose, and the people around us were there to bring us to that experience or guide us through it. The purpose will be different for each of us but, generally speaking, I believe it's something we're meant to learn and grow from to become the version of ourselves that we're meant to be. If we don't learn what we're supposed to and apply it, then we risk experiencing similar events again (and again) until we do.

My belief may seem fatalistic as it gives the sense that we have no choice in what we learn or are supposed to become. However, our experiences are based on choices. Erica, Helen, and Sam had the power to choose what to say, how to say it, and how to behave. I chose my reactions. The Boss and The Director chose theirs as well. And I believe that had any choice in this story been made differently, certain events could have been avoided or their impact lessened. Every event in this book was preventable. There are lessons here for all groups of people: management, teams and colleagues, and ourselves. Let's begin with ourselves.

ME

SIMPLY PUT, ALL of this started, and impacted me as much as it did, because of my attachments.

If I were to make a judgment about workplace attachments based solely on the experiences in this book, then I would have to say that they should be avoided. For example, be friendly but don't go beyond a professional relationship, and prioritize career over colleagues and feelings. If I had followed these beliefs, not only would I have had the healthy detachment needed to avoid my psychological meltdown, I'd also have been objective enough to leave the team in 2014, avoiding this experience entirely.

But this is a tricky one for me. I know that colleagues can become very good friends and some have found life partners through work. So, if I had to pick one of these two sides to be on, I would pick attachment. Despite how my own set me up for distress, there were others that brought me feelings of connectedness and belonging that made my work life more enjoyable than the job alone could have. However, knowing what I do now, there are some decisions I would make differently today.

Attachments and the workplace

There were three workplace attachments that got me into trouble: to The Boss, to the team, and to my job.

My attachment to The Boss was what started this whole mess for me. If I hadn't been so attached to him, I wouldn't have been as affected by his preference for the Number 2, nor felt so dependent on his good opinion to validate my skills or intelligence. Consequently, I doubt that I would have developed insomnia, which affected my ability to cope with what was happening around me, making me vulnerable to the attacks from Erica, Helen, and Sam. This attachment gave The Boss a power over me that he never should have had.

It isn't necessarily wrong to rely on another person's opinion of you to know if you're doing well. Career success, usually defined by career progression, isn't determined by your happiness with yourself or your work. Many workplaces have hierarchies and, if you want to move up in the hierarchy, you need someone above you to think well of you. Trying to fit into a mould that pleases your boss is one way of getting that, and it's normal to do that if you see that person as a mentor. I believed that if The Boss thought I was as smart or as skilled as him, then I'd have his appreciation and respect and could achieve the same success as he had.

But failing at this with a manager doesn't mean you failed as an employee. Sometimes you and your manager are just not a good fit with each other regarding how you work with, or what you need from, each other in the manager-employee relationship. Where The Boss was concerned, I sought validation from someone who liked a different kind of personality and type of experience and skill set than me – the textbook definition of *poor fit*. Excluding me from conversations with the Number 2 and not thinking of me as someone who could carry out my own research ideas were red flags. However, recognizing poor fit requires enough objectivity and detachment that you're able to step back and look at both of you critically. Because I idolized him as much as I did, and was attached to the image I had of who he *used* to be, I focused on trying to regain his good opinion instead of cutting my losses and moving on. When you recognize the differences in how you work and what you need from each other, it may be wise to find another employer or manager with whom you fit better, as you're then more likely to grow and succeed. This may mean walking away from the people, work, and environment that you enjoy.

This brings me to the second attachment that got me into trouble: the one with my team. Even if I realized that I was never going to fit with The Boss the way I wanted, I was attached enough to the camaraderie and friendship in the original crew that I wanted to stay. But people changed one by one over time, and each change shifted the team dynamic, but incrementally enough that those shifts were hard to notice. My attachment to what *used to be* kept me from seeing the shifts.

The first shift came from Erica's complaints about the Number 2. The first sign of it was how soon it was after meeting me that she started to complain about him. In my experience, most people who complain about someone do so to someone they know and trust, and Erica barely knew me.

This should have told me that she wasn't thoughtful about how openly she complained about someone, hinting at her willingness to damage someone publicly. The second sign was her unwillingness to accept advice on how to repair her relationship with him. At the time, I was inclined to believe her attempts failed because of her word and my own experiences with him, but I now question how much effort she put into working on the relationship versus just complaining about it.

What prevented me from seeing these signs? I assumed that anyone new would fit into the original dynamic, and it influenced my perceptions of Erica's behaviours such that I assumed she was someone who justifiably needed help instead of someone who was on a campaign. The lesson learned from this is to keep re-evaluating your environment. Take a step back occasionally to look at everyone around you, how you interact with each other, how they influence your choices and vice versa, and then assess whether what you see is the environment you want or the person you want to be in it. Never get so attached to a dynamic or relationship that you're unable to do that and see it for what it is in the present.

The second shift was how Louise was being treated. I am partially responsible for this and there are choices I regret making during this time, such as when I outed her in front of management for not completing her quality checks. I should have handled that by speaking privately with the new manager.

Another regrettable choice was not confronting Erica's unprofessional and mean remarks about Louise. I was responsible as her supervisor to tell her that her comments were inappropriate, but I didn't because of my growing detachment from Louise and my wish to protect a relationship with Erica. I saw Louise's behaviour and productivity issues as disruptive to the team dynamic. They encouraged so much frustration from myself, Erica, and others that I felt she needed to leave for the team to become whole again. I wasn't completely wrong: she was unhappy and needed a change. However, by detaching from her and attaching to those who were badmouthing her, I was socially excluding Louise, which was helping to ruin the team's friendly dynamic, not protect it. Even worse, I was allowing my frustration to blind me to the fact that I was attaching myself to people who thought social exclusion was okay. My attachment to Erica and a positive team dynamic also encouraged me to act more as a friend to her than as the supervisor I should have been. To this day, I'm not proud of myself for those choices and I don't want to make them again.

My attachment to my job was the third attachment that hindered me. The project represented everything I wanted to do at that agency and there was no other project there like it. I wanted to stay with what I enjoyed and found meaningful. This is a difficult attachment to address. We spend too many years working to afford being unhappy or unfulfilled. Many of us want to work on something we find meaningful and grow professionally. Even if you don't have that kind of a job, one that provides you with a good salary, benefits, and job security can be very difficult to move on from even if it's toxic. However, I was so attached to *everything* it could give me that I never thought about whether there were projects that could give me *some* of it. If I had, I could have prioritized what I wanted and found another position that would have given me what I wanted most.

Of course, there are practical aspects of sticking with a toxic job. I wouldn't advocate that someone gives up a good salary and benefits if they need to feed a family and don't have something just as good or better to turn to. However, I might suggest that they seek help to figure out how to put as much psychological distance as possible between themself and their co-workers without negatively impacting their position. A company's Employee Assistance Program or Informal Conflict Management service would be good resources to use. If it has neither, then I would recommend trying to find a free or affordable service that can provide practical guidance on maintaining professional relationships. If your company offers benefits, see if they cover psychological services as that might mitigate the cost of hiring a professional. You might also want to read books or journal articles related to toxic workplaces for guidance, or research the labour laws applicable to where you live to see what your rights are. I found the *Harvard Business Review* to be a good resource after I moved on and, in Canada, workers' rights are covered under the *Canada Labour Code* as well as under each province's or territory's own codes.

I might also have realized how my workload and poor relationship with Helen would stunt my professional development. I used to believe that being responsible for so much was good for me because I was learning valuable skills. However, it also prevented me from learning to lead and teach because I was too busy learning tasks on the fly and doing things myself. I was also unable to engage in developmental side projects because all my time was needed for the project. Further, Helen's unwavering support of Erica denied me the opportunity to learn how to manage a difficult employee. As much as I was improving my skill set, my knowledge base and leadership skills were being stunted. If I hadn't been as attached to what I was getting out of the project, I might have been able to step back and see the wider picture of what I was missing and needed to grow professionally.

Attachments to personae

Another attachment that harmed me was to the image of the person I thought I was and wanted to convey to those around me, as well as to pride. With a masters in social work degree, I had the education to recognize some of the team's ills and be the helper instead of the one who needed help. I also saw myself as strong and resilient enough to not let abusive behaviour drag me down; leaving the team would have meant admitting I was beaten and had run away. Finally, I had the third longest tenure of anyone on the team, and therefore had more than earned the right to outlast those who came after me. Obviously, that's not how things worked out. And, if I hadn't been attached to my pride or this image I had of myself, if I had allowed myself to shift, change, and show vulnerability earlier than I did, I might have been able to break all of my other attachments and exit this situation earlier.

Being a helper was just something I did, not something I consciously took on, and felt like the right thing to do. I never asked myself if I was doing the right thing by trying to be supportive of The Boss, by walking with Sam during lunch to help him decompress, by being patient with Erica or giving her the benefit of the doubt when she first turned on me. But there were two consequences: I spent energy on people who didn't believe they needed help, and focusing on them distracted me from realizing that I needed help myself.

I don't think I caused or worsened any issues on the team by trying to help those who didn't want it. If anything, it exposed me to the toxicity that I was surrounded by and, for Sam, gave me a preview of what was to come (even though I didn't realize that at the time). If I hadn't offered help, then I might be sitting here today wondering if being kinder would have made a difference and kicking myself for not having done more. But because everyone else's issues seemed so clear to me, and because I was the target of the aggression, I never took the time to look at how I got into the beaten-up insomniac position that I did, nor how my handling of it could have contributed to my own pain. As much as I knew that my insomnia, daily paranoia, and heightened alertness were not normal, I became used to them and resigned myself to remaining that way. This delayed me from getting the therapy I needed to improve my sleep, which delayed my ability to think more rationally about what was happening around me, thus delaying my realization that I needed to detach from the situation by leaving.

Working as hard on the project as I did also fed into why I didn't recognize that I needed help: I prioritized work, and regaining The Boss's favour, over my mental health. Work became a saviour of sorts, as it distracted me enough during the day to keep me from trancing and going down a deeper spiral, despite how it had brought me to that position in the first place. I also feared realizing that I wasn't as tough as I hoped and more flawed than I was willing to admit. This played a major role in why I didn't recognize my insomnia when it began and why it took me so long to seek help for it. Then, once I did and my sleep quality improved enough that I could think more rationally, I developed the confidence and strength to ask management for help with the toxic situation around me. Regrettably, this did not end well, but it taught me how high up the disregard for psychological safety was. Fortunately, by this time I had enough self-assuredness to know I deserved being treated better and had the strength to leave. If I hadn't been so attached to *appearing* strong, I might have actually *been* strong and made those moves sooner.

Finally, this feeds into how I was attached to the idea that my rank and tenure gave me the right to outlast my attackers. I haven't changed my opinion on this. I think years of loyal, hard-working service should count for something in the workplace, but that wasn't the environment I was in. Without that attachment, I might have left the team shortly after realizing I wouldn't get the support from Helen that I needed, or even sooner after seeing new people like the Number 2 and Sam being favoured by The Boss. I might have accepted the obvious sooner and left before things sank to the level they did.

Learning about myself

As much as I learned about who I wasn't, I learned something very important about who I am: an anxious person. Let me be clear about this: I sometimes find myself in situations where I feel anxious, but I do not live with anxiety. Those are two very different things, one having a neurological foundation that is lived with daily and for which some people require medication to manage, and the other being a state of mind that is triggered occasionally by certain situations and then leaves once the situation ends. I am in the latter category. I clarify this to prevent confusion about what I claim to be and so as not to expropriate from those who live with a very different challenge. This also comes from my own self-reflection and not a professional diagnosis.

I think I have been an anxious person for a long time, but I wasn't in tune with it before these events. For example, I prided myself on completing tasks quickly. This removed tasks from my mental to-do list and made me less likely to be blamed or deemed incompetent if the project became delayed. Instead, I was good at my job, productive, and reliable. I didn't recognize that anxiety underlay this.

As I wrote earlier, I never took time to reflect on this, partly because I didn't have the time but also because my anxiety was benefitting me. Why analyse what's working? But then feeling I lost The Boss's good opinion and my desire to regain it increased the anxiety I hadn't recognized, leading to my insomnia. Then came multiple attacks from multiple people. My need for self-preservation upped my already high anxiety even more, worsening my insomnia. It took two anxiety attacks for me to realize just how bad things were and to seek the help I needed to repair myself psychologically.

I'm much more in tune with this emotion now. I can identify it and am not afraid to share when I'm feeling it. I no longer believe that sharing it makes me look weak or vulnerable. In fact, I've found that doing so has been helpful because those I'm speaking with either then share that they also feel anxious, which validates all of us, or know better how to address my concerns. It's really about knowing who you are, what you need, and being able to communicate that openly and clearly. It's not rocket science, but I had to practice it, because I was so used to the walls I had long ago built to protect myself. Fortunately, the management I had in my new team provided the kind of environment where I felt I could experiment with showing vulnerability.

THE TEAM

I WASN'T THE only one who made poor choices. My experience provides lessons for teams and team management: fostering a psychologically healthy environment includes appreciating vulnerability and reaching out to employees when it appears something is wrong. I was too blinded by my issues with the Number 2 and Louise to recognize how unhealthy the team dynamic had become or how I'd contributed to it. I didn't recognize how Erica's behaviours, combined with how Sam chose to conceal his stress, were creating a psychologically unsafe work environment. What I don't know is if no one above me noticed it either, or if they simply didn't care.

I believe that the team manager is the primary person who can stop, or at least curb, toxic behaviour within a team. The manager has the authority and power to make necessary changes and can remain close enough to monitor the team environment. As I wrote, I barely spoke with Laura once I began reporting to Helen. She also didn't speak much with

Isaac or Erica, seemingly preferring to get all of her information about my side of the team from Helen. I'm not suggesting that Laura failed to prevent what happened or was irresponsible; she may not have known what was happening or appreciated the severity of it, and you can't act on what you don't know. However, if she didn't know, then I believe that is partially due to her not being engaged enough with the team to notice the gossiping, snide remarks, and the resulting tension regarding not just me but also Louise and Sam as well. Of course, the other part of that is my not informing her, which I didn't have the confidence to do because of our distant relationship and the doubts Helen had put in my head. Managers, you should be approachable and engaged with your teams. If you don't want to be, then don't manage a team. Even though Laura eventually left, she might have been able to make enough of an impact on the team atmosphere, or made changes in the team structure or management, to prevent the situation from worsening.

I realized how influential the manager can be after I joined my new team. There was a stark difference in management style between Laura and my new one. My new manager's desk was in the middle of everyone else's, whereas Laura opted to sit at the edge of the team's space. This influenced how close or distant I felt I was to either of them. More importantly, my new manager's openness about her mental health helped me feel I could safely share my own struggles because I knew she understood and could empathize. Plus, the fact that she had progressed as much as she did in her career despite those challenges told me that, professionally, there was still hope for me to progress and succeed in the agency.

My immediate supervisor also played a positive and meaningful role. She, too, made it clear that she valued mental health, which I saw in the constant openness and respectfulness that I felt from her. For example, whenever she shared information about a person or project that was not entirely positive, it was always done in a factual, respectful way with minimal detail. I knew I was with someone who would treat me respectfully both behind my back and to my face.

She also built a positive relationship with me by occasionally asking how I was doing and if there was anything she could do to support me. Looking back, I think that one reason why it was so easy for me to believe that I didn't have support was because no one in management ever asked me how I was. Laura never asked me about Helen's allegations against me, The Boss never followed up with me after the meeting with Sam, and The Director never asked me about my distance from The Boss when she first saw it. Any discussion I had with someone in management was initiated by me.

With that in mind, here are suggestions on how managers can help create and maintain a psychologically healthy team:

- Engage with your direct reports beyond the work. Make a point to say hello to them each day. Invite them individually for an occasional lunch or coffee break. Have weekly team meetings and spend the beginning of each talking about the weekend or anything personal they want to share with their colleagues. In short, make a point to get to know who they are and what's important to them, and let them get to know you. Creating and maintaining a positive familiarity with you will help them feel more comfortable approaching you if they need help. It might also help you ease into difficult conversations with them, should you ever need to, because you already have a strong foundation to begin that conversation from.

- But understand, and stick to, your professional role in relation to those who you work with. This goes beyond, but still includes, the typical workplace advice of being "friendly without being friends" and developing someone's potential without playing favourites. Anyone responsible for an employee must be impartial when difficult situations arise. In my case, Helen was far from impartial; I saw her as wanting to be Erica's champion, thereby enabling her toxic behaviour and preventing me from being able to manage her. If Helen had been more self-aware, impartial, and more of a supervisor to me than a champion to Erica, Erica's behaviour could have been addressed earlier and possibly tempered or stopped.

- That being written, I am guilty of the same, but in the opposite direction. My friendship with Erica encouraged me to give her a leeway in the beginning that, in retrospect, I shouldn't have. I don't regret giving her breathing space at the very start, but I should have started documenting her behaviours and my efforts to address them after that first conversation. Learn from me: be friendly and supportive of your staff, but remember that you're also responsible for them and you each have a role to play in relation to each other. Don't let friendship blind you to your role, nor be selective in whom you play that role with. Be impartial.

- Once you understand and commit to your role, make sure everyone else knows what it is. Make sure your employees are clear on what they can expect from you and that your management knows the same. In turn, you should be clear about what you expect from either of them. This obviously goes for work roles and responsibilities, but equally so for how you will choose to address issues of harassment, workplace violence, or other examples of toxicity in the workplace.

- And in those conversations about harassment, violence, and toxicity, as well as any conversations about mental health, I suggest going further by being clear about the kinds of conversations you will and will not have. I have been noticing more and more articles about psychological well-being in the workplace and the role managers can play. I read that managers should ensure that employees have the psychological support they need to perform well, and sometimes those readings include knowing how to listen and show empathy. They provide good advice and I appreciate the direction they're encouraging managers to take when speaking with an employee who needs support. However, not everyone is capable of listening to these stories or showing empathy.

- Some managers are incapable because they don't care, while for others it's because they're overloaded with their own mental health challenges and don't have the psychological space to hear or help with someone else's. Regardless, be clear with your employees that you cannot be the shoulder to cry on and, if they need help, what resources are available for them to turn to. If your own management expects you to be an empathetic listener, then be clear with them about your limitations, even though they might not appreciate hearing it, because it's dishonest and disrespectful to the person who needs the empathetic ear to pretend you have one when you don't. It can feel humiliating to expose yourself in this way to someone only to find out by their reaction or inaction that they will not provide the support you hoped for. Respect your employees enough to direct them towards the person or service that you know will serve them better, while assuring them that you will honour any accommodations or access to work resources that they may need.

It can be hard to ask someone if they're okay. How will they react? Will they feel that I'm intruding? If our relationship is based on work, is it appropriate for me to ask this question? I have these hang-ups as much as anyone else, particularly with those I don't work with directly or feel close to, and even more so with someone who's above me on the corporate ladder. However, if we want to create a work atmosphere that values good mental health and psychological safety, then we need to get over them: learn that it's acceptable to ask someone if they're okay, and how to do so while showing we respect whatever personal boundaries they may have. Yes, we need mental health training, but we will never get to put it to use if we hesitate to talk about it.

THE AGENCY

THOUGH THE LESSONS I write about in this section deal with the particular agency I was at, I believe they can apply to any workplace, public or private, small or large. I hope that anyone reading this will find an idea that can apply to where they work.

True, long-lasting change starts at the top. Why? First, no matter how good an idea is or how hard someone pushes an initiative, whether it's adopted and supported is decided by upper management. Second, people often learn to treat people based on how they have been treated themselves. Bullies aren't a homogenous group. Some use and abuse others for professional gain, don't care about the impact their actions have on their colleagues, or simply get a thrill from knowing that they have power over someone else's career. However, some managers will harass or treat others poorly because they themselves are being bullied or because their work culture is teaching them that it is acceptable. Those who treat their employees better in such an environment should be commended for bucking what their managers have created and being the positive leaders that their own won't be. It takes a good deal of self-confidence and conviction to behave differently.

In that vein, upper management can help create a psychologically healthy environment by modelling the behaviours they want to see in their employees: they can call out toxic behaviour when they see it, ask "How are you?" when they suspect something is wrong, and publicly acknowledge good work. It can also include implementing and promoting programs that demonstrate the values behind those behaviours, and ensuring they have the human and financial resources to run effectively.

And from that psychologically healthy environment, managers can create a psychologically *supportive* one. By that, I mean a management philosophy that goes beyond talking about respectfulness and empathy to one that actively offers help to those who are facing difficulties in the workplace, as well as offering professional resources and promoting their use. Without the modelling and the presence of obvious supports, employees are forced to decipher on their own – perhaps without any clues to guide them – whether it is wise or risky to voice their concerns and ask for help. I have heard managers say that it's the employee's responsibility to do this. I agree with that to an extent: you can't help someone who doesn't want to be helped, nor can management act on what it doesn't know. However, when it comes to harassment and workplace violence, particularly when those causing or enabling it have power over the employee being subjected to it, the employee is risking retaliation by voicing it. Employees need to weigh the benefit of what they hope they'll get against what they think is realistic and what it may cost them, a very difficult thing to do if you don't know what the manager's reaction will be.

Counteracting those fears is why it's important for management to model the behaviours I mentioned and effectively implement the programs that will help employees feel comfortable coming forward. Employees shouldn't feel as though they have nothing to lose before thinking it's worth speaking out. We need to create an environment where employees don't feel isolated, fear retribution, or believe that help isn't available. Here are two ideas on what companies can do to help create a psychologically supportive environment:

- Provide mental health first aid training

  Mental health first aid is designed to educate people about the most common types of mental illnesses out there, plus how to recognize when someone might be having trouble with their mental health, open a conversation with them about it, and to direct them to the support they need. It does not train people to be counsellors, nor should people who take this training believe it makes them one. However, it can give people the tools to show someone that at least one person in the workplace cares enough to notice something is wrong and to offer help. This could go a long way in breaking down the isolation someone can feel when they're dealing with a difficult situation, and help them connect with the support they need.

- Provide a floor ombudsperson

  Many companies have ombudspeople, but they work for

the organization at large. This doesn't take away from the good work that many of them do, but some employees may not feel comfortable reaching out to someone they don't know or believe won't understand their immediate work environment. Others may not have the emotional energy to explain the people and environment they're dealing with to someone who doesn't know.

The floor ombudsperson could resolve both of these issues. By working on the same floor as the employee, the ombudsperson would likely be familiar to them and know the environment they're working in. This familiarity can help some employees come forward because they would know that the ombudsperson already understands the environment and possibly the people they're dealing with, thereby reducing their need to explain everything from the top and relive the emotions along with it. A shared understanding, even if only a limited one, is already there.

The ombudsperson could be another employee on that floor who adopted the role on a volunteer basis (with appropriate training). They could report to an organizational ombudsperson or another individual certified to work in counselling, Informal Conflict Management, or similar. The floor ombudsperson wouldn't manage conflict or be a therapist, as that should be left to professionals with the appropriate certifications, but those professionals can advise the ombudsperson on how to guide an employee who comes to them for help.

The floor ombudsperson would be a neutral person who, like the person trained in mental health first aid, guides the employee to the type of help they need. However, this help would be related to conflict, harassment, or violence in the workplace instead of strictly to mental health issues. The ombudsperson could guide the employee to union assistance if the workplace is unionized, to an outside government authority, or to Labour Relations. They could also advocate on behalf of an employee to management when difficulties arise or be with the employee when they need to speak with management but feel they cannot do it alone.

Of course, these ideas are in addition to the external supports some workplaces have, such as Employee Assistance Programs (EAP) or Informal Conflict Management services. The EAP counsellors are trained professionals who work outside of the company, some of whom have private practices, and are paid by the company to provide employees the psychological help they need to either keep working or return to work. There is typically a maximum number of sessions or hours an employee can use for free.

Informal Conflict Management is similar in that it is free to the employee and the professionals are not company employees. However, their focus is more on helping employees manage conflict or difficult relationships at work, or mediating between employees if they're unable to work together harmoniously.

Both EAP and Informal Conflict Management helped me immensely. I hope your workplace has them and, if not, that you can access low-cost professional services or have health coverage that will cover them. The skilled help that a certified, trained professional can provide complements, yet goes well beyond, what the friendly face on the floor can do.

Some people who commit harassment or workplace violence, or are generally disrespectful towards others, can benefit from these services as well. I wrote that some people bully because of how they have been treated. There are also people who bully because they're lashing out as a way of dealing (albeit inappropriately) with a difficult personal situation or mental health challenge of their own. Such individuals are not necessarily bullies by nature, but by circumstance, and can change for the better with the appropriate support.

However, these ideas will only go so far if employees fear or are uncomfortable speaking with management. I repeat: *positive and meaningful change needs to come from the top and be modelled.* The suggestions I wrote for managers in the previous section apply equally to Directors or CEOs.

I will close this section by first reiterating how I began it: none of these suggestions will bear fruit if management doesn't support them, and support includes giving the service or program the human and financial resources to run effectively, believing in its objective, and wanting to contribute to its success. Unfortunately, some of us have managers who choose to remain ignorant. In my experience, I saw this when The Boss told me that he didn't want to discuss what happened on the team, saying it would only be a rehash, and when The Director told me I was "heard" when I described the toxic behaviours on the team and offered suggestions on how to prevent similar situations. To me, both examples show wilful ignorance and a lack of leadership.

If you find yourself in a situation like this, you have some tough decisions to make. You can choose to stay and accept that you will not be supported, try to find someone else in management who will help you, or leave your job. None of these solutions feels good, so you need to pick the one you think you can live the easiest with. For myself, I chose to leave, stay gone, and engaged EAP and Informal Conflict Management services to help me. My ending was regrettable but I don't regret my choices. It was much easier for me to live with how it ended than how it would have been if I had chosen to stay but not to fight. However, that's me, and you may prefer a different path or have reason to believe that your outcome will be different.

These ideas are only a start to the conversation. I share them in the hopes that, if implemented, they can make a positive difference for someone, or that they can lead to even better ideas.

FINAL THOUGHTS

MY VOICE IS just one of many from people who have experienced harassment or violence in the workplace. I don't know many others who had experiences similar to mine, but I've read enough in the media and in workplace literature to know that I am not unique. This book isn't meant to break the subject wide open, but rather to document what some of these behaviours can look like and how they can impact someone. I hope that raising awareness of this will lead to more people being understanding and empathetic with someone who is dealing with this, as well as motivated to intervene when they see such behaviours occur. If you are one of those people who is experiencing something similar now or did in the past, I hope this book validates at least some of the thoughts and feelings you might have been dealing with. I hope you feel less alone.

And if you see yourself in one of the people who committed the violence in this book, then I hope you saw how damaging that can be to the other person. I also hope you're choosing to do better and get the support you need to do that.

ACKNOWLEDGEMENTS

This book would not have been possible without the support of a certain few people around me. One of them is editor Wayne Jones. He took me on and offered very helpful critiques for my first and second drafts. I'm still far from being a skilled story-teller, but I've learned a lot from his advice and edits. I hope I'm a better writer now than I was when I began this process.

I also want to thank two former co-workers of mine who supported me throughout the events of this book: one while they were happening, and the other as I was trying to recover from them. They heard me – repeatedly – rant and rave over the latest twists and turns, lament over my disappointments and losses, and try to make sense of it all. You were incredibly patient with me.

Thank you also to everyone I worked with before, during, and after the events in this book who were examples of what kind and professional co-workers are. Without you before these events, I might not have known what a healthy workplace was supposed to look like, believing that these types of events and behaviours were normal. Without you during, I wouldn't have had people to escape to in brief conversations while getting my morning tea or refilling the social committee canteen, providing me with momentary reprieves from the toxicity I was surrounded by. Without you after, I wouldn't have had people to restore my faith in teamwork.

Of course, my mental health professionals played a significant role in my recovery as well. They each gave me a safe outlet for my emotions and returned with some very helpful advice and coping techniques. I particularly want to thank the psychologist who gave me the plan to get my sleep back on track: once that happened, everything around me started to look so much clearer.

Finally, I want to thank my husband and daughter, without whose patience and cooperation I wouldn't have been able to write this book. It took me MUCH longer to write than I would have liked, but it would have been longer if I wasn't able to take the time at night to pound away at it while my husband and daughter played computer games together upstairs. This was when him being "the fun parent" was very helpful to me. I hope it continues because I'm not done writing.

www.ingramcontent.com/pod-product-compliance
Lightning Source LLC
Chambersburg PA
CBHW030516210326
41597CB00013B/927